My FIRST RECIPE BOOK

RECIPES FOR THE FOOD
KIDS REALLY WANT TO MAKE (AND EAT)

RICARDO

Library and Archives Canada Cataloguing in Publication is available upon request.

ISBN: 978-0-525-61250-6

eBook ISBN: 978-0-525-61251-3

Printed in China

The authorized representative in the EU for product safety and compliance is Penguin Random House Ireland, Morrison Chambers, 32 Nassau Street, Dublin D02 YH68, Ireland, https://eu-contact.penguin.ie

Published in Canada by Appetite by Random House®, a division of Penguin Random House Canada Limited.
320 Front Street West, Suite 1400
Toronto, Ontario, M5V 3B6, Canada
penguinrandomhouse.ca

10 9 8 7 6 5 4 3 2 1

Penguin
Random House
Canada

THE RICARDO TEAM

Chef and Author: Ricardo
Directors — Content and Creation: Maude Bourcier-Bouchard and Myriam Huzel (interim)
Studio Director — Creation and Production: Josée Berniqué
Art Director: Cristine Berthiaume
Recipe Development: Etienne Marquis, Alexane Labonté, Laurence Viens, Nicolas Cadrin and Kareen Grondin
Recipe Tester: Danielle Bessette
Editor: Marie-Pier Gagnon
Translation: Vicki Karigiannis and Michelle Diamond
Photographers: David de Stefano and Jean-Michel Poirier
Graphic Designer: Michèle Hénen
Food Stylists: Nataly Simard and Etienne Marquis
Accessories Stylist: Sylvain Riel, Caroline Nault and Geneviève Larocque
Photo Retouching: David de Stefano and Jean-Michel Poirier
Graphic Artists: Karine Breton, Mathieu Lafontaine and Ève Paquet
Illustrations: Michèle Hénen and Jacques Laplante
Project Manager — Projects and Production: Marisol Moquin Laferrière
Project Manager: Martine Lauriault
Studio and Traffic Coordinator: Josianne Monette
Recipe Revision: Louise Faucher
Photo Archives: Maude Chauvin, David de Stefano, Dana Dorobantu, Christian Lacroix and Jean-Michel Poirier
Getty images: Hakase_, filmstudio, fizkes and Chong Kee Siong

President: Brigitte Coutu
General Director: Mireille Arteau
Vice-President Communications and Marketing: Nathalie Carbonneau

ricardocuisine.com

Caution to grown-ups

No one is better suited than you to know whether your child needs supervision when making the recipes in this book. Be they teenagers or little children, young cooks must be aware at all times of the risk of accidents that can occur in the kitchen: knives, boiling water, oven, hot oil, etc. For this reason, we recommend adult supervision during recipe preparation and disclaim all responsibility in the case of any incident.

TABLE OF CONTENTS

01
BREAKFAST IS MORE THAN JUST CEREAL!

02
FOR BIG & SMALL CRAVINGS

03
SO... WHAT ARE WE EATING?!

04

I'M THIRSTY!

05

YOUR FAVORITE CHAPTER: DESSERTS

WHO IS {RICARDO?}

HE'S A CANADIAN CHEF, COOKBOOK AUTHOR, FATHER OF THREE...
AND HE HAS THE SWEETEST TOOTH IN THE WHOLE WIDE WORLD!

Who taught you how to cook?
Both my mom and grandmother inspired me in the kitchen, but I also taught myself.

Why do you cook?
Because I love seeing the look of happiness on my loved ones' faces when they eat my food!

Do you have a tip for someone who's just starting to cook?
Stay curious and don't give up when something goes differently than you planned.

What's your favorite recipe in this book?
Burger Tacos (p. 94)!

What's your favorite style of international food?
East and Southeast Asian cuisine, because I love the combination of sweet and salty flavors!

What was your biggest cooking disaster?
I was making pike quenelles (they're like a fish meatball), and I tried shaping them at night for a photoshoot the next day but I couldn't get the texture right and they just fell apart. This was 25 years ago, and the internet was still new so there wasn't a place for me to look it up and understand where I went wrong.

What dish do you love making for your daughters?
General Tso's chicken. Be sure to try my tofu version (it's just as tasty!) on page 115.

What cooking technique still gives you trouble?
Cooking the perfect steak.

What do you often tell yourself while cooking?
I tell myself not to worry if a dish isn't perfect; I'm not performing open heart surgery!

What's your favorite food?
All the desserts! Cake, lemon pie, mille-feuille (a layered dessert with puff pastry and cream), to name just a few!

What's the one food you would want with you on a deserted island?
Potatoes, because they're so versatile. I could make fries, chips, mashed potatoes...

What's the one food you don't like to eat?
Veal liver!

What was your favorite dish when you were a kid?
Pâté chinois, which is a French-Canadian type of shepherd's pie.

Which recipe do you usually fail at making?
Maple fudge. It never quite turns out like my mom's.

What's the weirdest food you've ever eaten?
The heads of huge shrimp!

YOUR BOOK

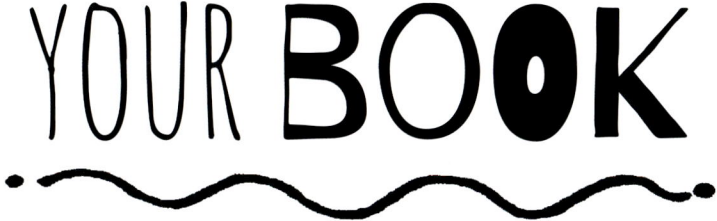

The book you're holding in your hands right now doesn't belong to me—even though my name's on the front! It doesn't belong to the grown-ups in your life either. It belongs to *you*, and you alone. (Unless you're sharing with a sibling...) You can do whatever you want with it: you can read it from back to front; you can dip in and out; you can get the pages dirty; you can fold the corners of your favorite pages; you can even keep it closed if you've memorized a recipe already!

My dream is that this book will make you want to cook often, discover new dishes and develop new skills. Maybe you'll even try (and like!) a few foods you always thought you hated. (Broccoli isn't so bad, I promise!) But what's most important is that you have *fun* cooking and baking.

I know for certain that this book can make that happen, and you're capable of making every recipe that I handpicked just for you. You'll be so proud of yourself when you pull it off! And it's never too soon to start when it comes to cooking.

Have fun and bon appétit!

RICARDO

in the school cafeteria with
YOUR FRIENDS

Sunday evenings with
YOUR GRANDPARENT

Saturday mornings with
YOUR SIBLING

{ EATING TOGETHER }
IS WHAT COUNTS THE MOST

WE LOVE SITTING DOWN FOR A TASTY MEAL, BUT
IN THE END, IT'S TIME SPENT AT THE TABLE SURROUNDED
BY LOVED ONES THAT WE'LL CHERISH EVEN MORE.

going on a picnic with
YOUR COUSINS

Tuesday nights with
YOUR PARENT

one-on-one with
YOUR BESTIE

WHY? WHY? WHY?

HI! MY NAME'S QUENTIN ALEXANDER (my friends call me Q&A) and I have a few questions.

WHEN I'M COOKING, I ALWAYS HAVE LOTS OF QUESTIONS, AND RICARDO HELPS ME GET THE ANSWERS I NEED. FOLLOW ME ALONG THROUGHOUT THIS BOOK AND WE CAN LEARN TOGETHER.

HOW CAN I STAY SAFE IN THE KITCHEN?

Most importantly, always have an adult nearby and ask for help when you need it. Always wash hands before and after cooking; this is to make sure the food remains safe to eat. When using knives, keep fingers tucked away and only cut on a stable surface with the help of an adult. Clean up any spills that happen as you go to prevent slipping.

Also, it's essential to remember the following when cooking in the oven or on the stove: always use oven mitts to touch hot pans (ouch!), and never ever leave the stove unattended. Keep kitchen towels and other items away from the heat so they don't catch fire. Turn pot handles inward so they don't accidentally get knocked over. And don't forget to turn off the stove and oven when you're done!

WHY DO FRUITS AND VEGGIES NEED TO BE WASHED?

Even if you plan to peel them, you need to wash fruits and veggies. Why? Because germs on the outside can stick to your knife or peeler and transfer them to the inside (gross!). Always scrub your fruits and veggies under running water, and if you're not peeling them, you can even use a brush to clean them. (A vegetable brush, silly, not your toothbrush!)

WHAT ARE THE DIFFERENT NUMBERS USED IN THE RECIPES?

There are two systems of measurements that exist: metric and imperial. The metric system uses units like meters, liters and grams. It's measured by tens (for example, 10 millimeters = 1 centimeter, and 100 centimeters = 1 meter), so it's very easy to multiply or divide. The imperial system, however, doesn't have a simple pattern: it uses inches, feet, ounces, pounds and cups, and, for example, 12 inches = 1 foot, but 16 ounces = 1 pound. Different countries use different systems, and I included both in this book so you can cook along wherever you are!

WHY SHOULD I FOLLOW A RECIPE?

To make a recipe perfectly, it helps to follow the steps carefully. The recipes in this book were tested in the kitchen many times to make sure they always turn out great. Read the whole recipe first, and make sure you have everything you need before starting. Of course, you can add more of what you love to suit your taste. (After all, who doesn't love extra bacon in their Caesar salad?) But for desserts, it's important to follow the recipe exactly—otherwise, you might end up with a flat cake or runny ice cream!

GOING TO THE
GROCERY STORE

GRAB A CART AND JOIN ME IN THE AISLES
OF THE GROCERY STORE. I HAVE A FEW TIPS TO HELP YOU
FIGURE THINGS OUT NEXT TIME YOU'RE THERE!

FRESHNESS LIMIT

BEST BEFORE 05/12/2028

On all packaged foods, you'll see a best before date. This tells you when it will stop tasting as good. Always check the date before buying so you don't end up with a huge container of yogurt you need to eat *really* fast!

RIPE FOR THE PICKING

Sometimes fruits and veggies are still hard or green when you buy them, but they should ripen over a few days on your kitchen counter. Next time you shop, feel the fruit or veggie (without pressing too hard!) to check that it's not too hard or too soft. Also, check if it has, smooth skin and no bruises.

WHERE DOES IT COME FROM?

If you want to know where a fruit or vegetable comes from, just look at the little sticker on it and it will tell you the country of origin! It's a great way to find out whether your food comes from Canada, the US or somewhere else, because it's always best to buy from local farmers when you can.

CHECK THE LIST

1

The ingredients list on food packages tells you everything that's inside. The ingredients are listed in order from the most to the least. So if "oats" is listed first on a box of chewy bars, it means there are more oats than anything else in it.

2

If you see a word that ends in "-ose," it's a type of sugar. Examples are sucrose, fructose, saccharose, glucose and more.

SUGAR

ADDITIVES

3

Pick foods that have lists with fewer strange-sounding words, as the ones you can't pronounce (sodium ascorbate?!?) are usually additives. Fewer additives mean the food is likely something close to what you would make at home!

ALLERGENS

4

If you have allergies, check the list for the main allergens like peanuts, tree nuts or eggs. They're always clearly listed and easy to spot to help keep you safe.

CHAPTER 01

BREAKFAST
IS MORE THAN JUST CEREAL!

Is your breakfast feeling a bit boring with the usual peanut butter and milk every day? It doesn't have to! Here are a few fun recipes to make your morning routine super special and way more exciting!

The ultimate wake-up call

Breakfast Banana Split

REPLACE THE ICE CREAM WITH VANILLA GREEK YOGURT AND THEN ADD GRANOLA. TALK ABOUT A BALANCED BREAKFAST!

preparation 10 minutes / **serving** 1

⅓ cup	(75 ml) granola of your choice (recipes p. 23 and p. 24)
1	medium ripe banana, halved lengthwise
½ cup	(125 ml) vanilla Greek yogurt (see Yummy Yogurt and As You Like It p. 19)
½ cup	(70 g) fresh berries (such as raspberries, blueberries, blackberries)
⅓ oz	(10 g) dark chocolate or milk chocolate
1	fresh cherry (optional)

1 Place the granola in an oval-shaped bowl. Place the banana halves lengthwise on either side of the granola.

2 Top the granola with the yogurt in three mounds. Garnish with the berries.

3 Hold a piece of chocolate or a chocolate bar in one hand and a vegetable peeler in the other hand. Peel the chocolate on its thinnest side to get small chocolate shavings.

4 Decorate the banana split with the chocolate shavings and the cherry. Serve immediately.

YUMMY YOGURT

Greek yogurt is just regular yogurt that's been strained to make it super thick and creamy. It's packed with protein, which will keep your belly full at breakfast and help you stay full until lunchtime.

EGGS-PONENTIAL INCREASE

You can double or even quadruple this recipe, no problem! Just remember to use two eggs for each person. Also, use a larger pan if you're cooking lots of eggs.

Scrambled Eggs with Bell Pepper and Cheese

PUT SOME PEP INTO YOUR SCRAMBLED EGGS BY ADDING VEGGIES AND CHEESE. IT'S QUICK, EASY AND TASTES EGG-CELLENT!

- -

preparation 10 minutes / **cooking** 6 minutes
serving 1

2	eggs
1	green onion, chopped
¼	red bell pepper, seeded and diced
1 tbsp	butter
2 tbsp	grated mozzarella or mild cheddar cheese

1 In a bowl, beat the eggs and green onion well with a fork. Season with salt and pepper.

2 In a small non-stick skillet over medium heat, soften the bell pepper in the butter. Add the egg mixture and cook for 2 minutes, stirring often with a wooden spoon or spatula. Add the cheese and let melt for 1 minute. Stir and serve immediately.

A FLURRY OF FLAKES

This granola uses two types of oats! Quick oats, which stick together in little clumps, and old-fashioned oats, which are large and stay separate. The result? A granola that's super easy to sprinkle on your yogurt for a tasty treat!

Crunchy Granola

YOGURT WITH GRANOLA? LOVE THAT "CRUNCH, CRUNCH" SOUND WHEN YOU'RE EATING YOUR MORNING YOGURT? GOOD NEWS: IT NEVER HAS TO END.

preparation 15 minutes / **cooking** 30 minutes
cooling 1 hour / **makes about** 5 cups (1.25 L)

½ cup	(125 ml)	plain yogurt
½ cup	(125 ml)	maple syrup
¼ cup	(60 ml)	vegetable oil
1½ cups	(150 g)	old-fashioned/large flake oats
1½ cups	(150 g)	quick cook oats
½ cup	(80 g)	pumpkin seeds
½ cup	(55 g)	sliced almonds
½ cup	(35 g)	coconut shavings
¼ tsp		salt

1 With the rack in the middle position, preheat the oven to 350°F (180°C). Line a baking sheet with a silicone mat or parchment paper.

2 In a large bowl, combine the yogurt, maple syrup and oil. Add both types of oats and mix well. Let sit for 5 minutes to let the oats absorb the liquid. Stir in the remaining ingredients. Spread the mixture out on the baking sheet.

3 Bake for 25 minutes. Gently flip the granola over. Continue to bake for 5 minutes or until the granola is nicely browned. Remove from the oven and let cool completely on the baking sheet, about 1 hour.

4 The granola will keep for 1 month in an airtight container at room temperature.

Rice Cereal Granola

CUSTOMIZE RICE CEREAL GRANOLA BY ADDING DRIED FRUIT, CHOCOLATE CHIPS OR EVEN SHREDDED COCONUT. THE POSSIBILITIES ARE ENDLESS!

preparation 15 minutes / **cooking** 30 minutes
cooling 1 hour / **makes about** 5 cups (1.25 L)

2 cups	(200 g) old-fashioned/large flake oats
2 cups	(60 g) crispy rice cereal (Rice Krispies–style) (see As Long as It's Crunchy)
½ cup	(80 g) pumpkin seeds
½ cup	(75 g) sunflower seeds
¼ tsp	salt
½ cup	(125 ml) maple syrup
¼ cup	(60 ml) vegetable oil
	Toppings of your choice: dried fruit, chocolate chips, grated coconut, etc.

1 With the rack in the middle position, preheat the oven to 325°F (165°C). Line a baking sheet with a silicone mat or parchment paper.

2 In a large bowl, combine the oats, rice cereal, pumpkin seeds, sunflower seeds and salt. Add the maple syrup and oil. Mix well. Spread the mixture out on the baking sheet.

3 Bake for 30 minutes, stirring every 10 minutes. Remove from the oven and let cool completely on the baking sheet, about 1 hour.

4 Add toppings, if desired. The granola will keep for 1 month in an airtight container at room temperature.

AS LONG AS IT'S CRUNCHY

You can replace the crispy rice cereal with either puffed rice or puffed quinoa. As long as it's crunchy, it'll still taste great!

Smoothie Bowl

THICKER THAN A SMOOTHIE, YOU'LL NEED A SPOON TO EAT THIS! SERVED IN A BOWL, LIKE A BREAKFAST SOUP, BUT YOU DON'T NEED TO BLOW ON IT TO COOL IT DOWN.

preparation 15 minutes / **serving** 1

½ cup	(125 ml) plain Greek yogurt
⅓ cup	(50 g) frozen blueberries (see Fresh or Frozen)
⅓ cup	(45 g) fresh blackberries
½	small banana, sliced into rounds
1 tbsp	(15 ml) maple syrup
⅓ cup	(75 ml) granola of your choice (recipes p. 23 and opposite)

1 In a personal blender (see Glossary p. 192) fitted with the blending blade, purée the yogurt, three-quarters of the fruit and the maple syrup until smooth. Pour into a small bowl.

2 Top with the remaining fruit and the granola.

FRESH OR FROZEN

You can definitely replace frozen blueberries with fresh ones. If you do, be sure to put your smoothie in the fridge for a few minutes to cool it down before digging in. It'll taste even better.

HOT DOGS FOR
BREAKFAST?

Breakfast Hot Dogs

WAKE UP TO BREAKFAST SAUSAGE, EGG AND MELTY CHEESE IN A HOT DOG BUN. DREAMS REALLY DO COME TRUE!

preparation 20 minutes / **cooking** 12 minutes
servings 6

6	breakfast sausages
3 tbsp	butter
3	eggs
6	hot dog buns
½ cup	(50 g) grated mozzarella cheese
3	slices cooked bacon, halved crosswise
2	green onions, thinly sliced (optional)

TO COOK **YOUR BACON,** go to page 83.

1 With the rack in the middle position, preheat the oven to 375°F (190°C).

2 In a large non-stick skillet over medium-high heat, brown the sausages in 2 tbsp of the butter for 8 minutes, turning them over regularly. Set aside on a plate.

3 Meanwhile, in a bowl, beat the eggs well with a fork. Season with salt and pepper. Set aside.

4 In the same skillet, brown the unopened buns on each side. Add more butter as needed. Place the buns in an 11 × 8-inch (28 × 20 cm) baking dish. Open the buns and sprinkle the cheese inside. Bake for 3 to 4 minutes or until the cheese has melted.

5 Meanwhile, in the same skillet over medium heat, melt the remaining butter. Add the eggs and cook for 3 minutes, stirring often with a wooden spoon or spatula, until the eggs are just cooked. Remove the skillet from the heat. Season to taste.

6 Fill the buns with the sausages, bacon and scrambled eggs. Sprinkle with the green onions. Serve immediately.

Easy Microwave Omelet

IT'S SATURDAY MORNING AND YOU'RE RUNNING LATE FOR SOCCER PRACTICE OR GYMNASTICS LESSONS! GET YOUR ENERGY BOOST IN JUST A FEW MINUTES WITH A QUICK MICROWAVE OMELET! HERE ARE TWO FLAVOR VARIETIES TO CHOOSE FROM, USING THE SAME SIMPLE METHOD.

preparation 5 minutes / **cooking** 1 minute
serving 1

HAM OMELET

1	egg
3 tbsp	small-diced cooked ham
2 tbsp	grated cheddar cheese

PESTO AND TOMATO OMELET

1	egg
2 tbsp	small-diced tomato
2 tbsp	grated mozzarella cheese
½ tsp	(2.5 ml) pesto
½	green onion, chopped (optional)

1 In a microwave-safe shallow dish, combine all of the ingredients for your chosen omelet with a fork. Season with salt and pepper.

2 Cook the omelet in the microwave oven for 30 seconds. Open the door for 5 seconds. Close the door and continue to cook for 30 seconds (cooking the omelet in two stages gives it time to deflate and prevents it from splitting open as it cooks). The center of the omelet will still be slightly runny. Let rest for 1 minute.

3 Using a spatula, detach the omelet from the sides of the dish and slide onto a plate. Fold the omelet in half, if desired.

YOU CAN'T MAKE AN OMELET WITHOUT BREAKING A FEW EGGS

OOPS!

pesto and tomatoes

ham

Q&A TIME
WITH QUENTIN

WHY DO WE ADD VINEGAR TO WAFFLE BATTER?

When you mix milk with vinegar, you get the effect of buttermilk, which is thick and a bit tangy. Then, when you add baking soda, it makes the batter rise and cook up nice and fluffy. This chemical reaction is what makes your waffles thick and tasty. Hooray for science!

Super Fluffy Waffles

GET OUT THE WAFFLE IRON FROM THE BACK OF THE CUPBOARD AND MAKE SOME YUMMY WAFFLES. ONCE YOU START USING IT, YOU WON'T WANT TO STOP.

preparation 15 minutes / **cooking** 10 minutes
servings 4 / **freezes well**

¾ cup	(180 ml) milk
1 tsp	(5 ml) apple cider vinegar
1 cup	(150 g) unbleached all-purpose flour
3 tbsp	icing sugar
½ tsp	baking powder
½ tsp	baking soda
¼ tsp	salt
1 tbsp	(15 ml) vegetable oil
2	eggs

1 In a bowl, combine the milk and vinegar. Let sit for 5 minutes, until the mixture resembles buttermilk.

2 Meanwhile, preheat a waffle iron.

3 In a large bowl, whisk together the flour, icing sugar, baking powder, baking soda and salt.

4 Add the milk mixture, oil and eggs to the large bowl of dry ingredients. Mix well (a few lumps of flour will remain).

5 Pour about ⅓ cup (75 ml) of the waffle batter into each cavity of the waffle iron (or follow the manufacturer's instructions). Close the machine. Cook for 4 to 5 minutes or until the waffles are cooked through and golden. Keep the waffles warm in an oven preheated to 200°F (95°C) while you cook the remaining batter, or serve them as you go.

WEEKDAY BREAKFAST
You can freeze or refrigerate waffles. If you're running late for school, just pop a couple in the toaster.

{ CRUMB AND GET IT }

WHO HASN'T LEFT CRUSHED CEREAL PIECES AT THE BOTTOM OF THE BOX? LUCKILY, THERE ARE PLENTY OF FUN WAYS TO USE THEM UP.

BYE-BYE CEREAL WASTE!

Use your leftover cereal for...
> Quick and easy Rice Cereal Granola (p. 24)
> French Toast Rolls (p. 35)
> A party mix with nuts and dried fruit

WHICH CEREAL
SHOULD I GO WITH?

To make these rolls, you can use whatever cereal you have at home:

1 Crispy rice cereal like Rice Krispies
2 Toasted flaked corn cereal like Corn Flakes (but not the frosted kind!)
3 O-shaped oat cereal like Cheerios
4 Or get creative with a mix of your favorite cereals!

Cereal-Crusted French Toast Rolls

THESE SOFT AND CRISPY FRENCH TOAST ROLLS WILL HAVE YOU ROLLING OUT OF BED THE MOMENT YOU OPEN YOUR EYES.

preparation 30 minutes / **cooking** 8 minutes
servings 4

⅓ cup	(75 g) unsalted butter, softened
3 tbsp	brown sugar
1 tsp	ground cinnamon
8	slices white bread
1	egg
¼ cup	(60 ml) milk
1 cup	(30 g) mixed cereal (see Which Cereal Should I Go With? p. 34)
	Maple syrup, for serving

1 In a small bowl, combine 3 tbsp of the butter, the brown sugar and the cinnamon with a fork until the texture is spreadable.

2 On a work surface, cut the crusts off the bread. Save the crusts for another use (for example: breadcrumbs). Using a rolling pin, flatten the slices of bread.

3 Spread the butter mixture over the flattened bread. Roll the slices up into logs. Set aside on a plate.

4 In a shallow dish, combine the egg and milk with a fork. In a second shallow dish, coarsely crush the cereal.

5 Dip 1 French toast roll at a time in the egg mixture, letting some of the excess drip off. Gently press into the cereal to coat well.

6 In a large non-stick skillet over medium heat, brown the rolls in the remaining butter, turning them over regularly, until nicely browned. Serve the French toast rolls with maple syrup.

EVEN BETTER WITH PLENTY OF MAPLE SYRUP!

Chocolate Pancakes

THE THICKER THE PANCAKE, THE BETTER! SO THICK IT'S PRACTICALLY A CAKE THAT'S BEEN COOKED IN A PAN. GET IT? PAN-CAKE!

preparation 20 minutes / **cooking** 20 minutes
servings 4

¾ cup	(115 g) unbleached all-purpose flour
3 tbsp	cocoa powder
2 tbsp	sugar
1½ tsp	baking powder
¼ tsp	baking soda
¼ tsp	salt
¾ cup	(180 ml) milk
1 tbsp	(15 ml) white vinegar or lemon juice
1	egg
2 tbsp	(30 ml) vegetable oil
1 tsp	(5 ml) vanilla
2 oz	(55 g) milk chocolate chips or chopped chocolate
	Softened butter, for cooking

1 In a bowl, combine the flour, cocoa powder, sugar, baking powder, baking soda and salt.

2 In a large bowl, combine the milk and vinegar. Let sit for 5 minutes, until the mixture resembles buttermilk. Add the egg, oil and vanilla. Whisk to combine. Whisk in the dry ingredients until the mixture is smooth. Stir in the chocolate.

3 Heat a large non-stick skillet or crepe pan over medium heat. Once the skillet is hot, brush with butter.

4 Cook three pancakes at a time, using 3 tbsp (45 ml) of batter for each one, for 3 minutes. The pancakes are ready to flip over when bubbles start to form at the center or when the edges are starting to cook. Adjust the heat as needed to allow the pancakes time to cook before they brown too quickly.

5 Continue to cook on the second side for 1 minute or until the pancakes are cooked through and golden. Keep the pancakes warm in an oven preheated to 200°F (95°C) while you cook the remaining batter, or serve them as you go.

CHAPTER 02

FOR
BIG & SMALL CRAVINGS

"GROOOOOWL!" WHEN YOUR TUMMY RUMBLES AS LOUD AS A HUNGRY MONSTER, YOU KNOW IT'S TIME TO EAT! THESE SNACKS WILL SATISFY YOUR APPETITE AFTER SCHOOL OR DURING A FEROCIOUS HUNGER PANG ANY TIME.

Warm Broccoli and Cheddar Dip

BELIEVE IT OR NOT, THIS CHEESY DIP WILL ACTUALLY HAVE YOU BEGGING TO EAT MORE VEGGIES. BRING ON THE BROCCOLI!

preparation 15 minutes / **cooking** 5 minutes
makes 1½ cups (375 ml)

2 cups	(140 g) broccoli florets (see Food Waste Tip)
½	garlic clove, peeled
½ block	(4½ oz/125 g) cream cheese, softened
½ cup	(50 g) grated sharp cheddar cheese

1 In a small pot of salted boiling water, cook the broccoli and garlic until tender. Drain.

2 In a food processor, chop the broccoli and garlic. Add both types of cheese and purée until smooth. During this step, stop the food processor and remove the lid. Using a spatula, scrape down the sides of the food processor. Replace the lid and continue to mix. Season with salt and pepper.

3 Transfer the mixture to a glass bowl. Heat in the microwave oven for 30 seconds to 1 minute or until the dip is hot. Mix well.

4 Serve the dip with vegetable crudités or crackers. The dip will keep for 1 week in an airtight container in the refrigerator. Reheat and mix well before serving.

FOOD WASTE TIP

Don't throw out those broccoli stems! Peel them and enjoy them raw with your dip.

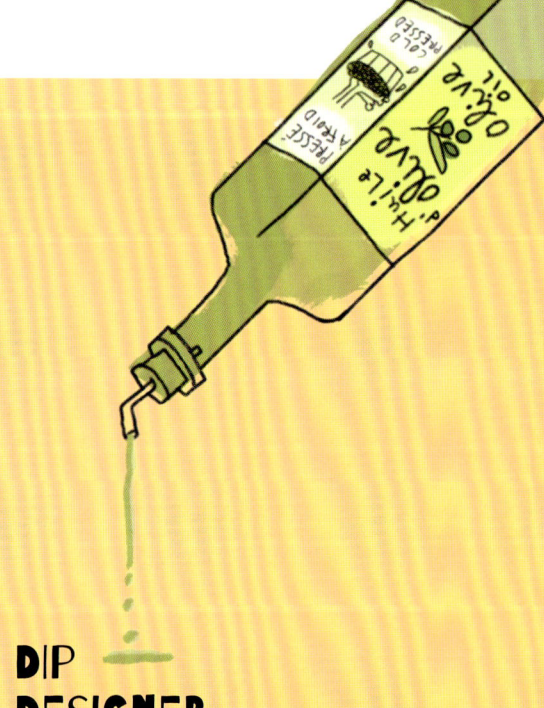

DIP DESIGNER

Be sure to save some chickpeas for decoration! If you forget, just garnish your dip with a sprinkle of curry powder, some chopped herbs and a drizzle of olive oil!

Hummus

IT'S THE ALL-PURPOSE DIP YOU WON'T WANT TO GO WITHOUT! YOU CAN DIP YOUR VEGGIES AND PITA CHIPS IN IT, OR EVEN SPREAD SOME IN A SANDWICH.

preparation 15 minutes / **makes about** 1¾ cups (430 ml)

1 can	(19 oz/540 ml) chickpeas, rinsed and drained
1	small garlic clove, peeled
¼ cup	(60 ml) water
3 tbsp	(45 ml) olive oil, plus more for serving
2 tbsp	(30 ml) lemon juice
1 tbsp	finely chopped flat-leaf parsley
1 tsp	sesame seeds (optional)
1	pinch sweet paprika

1 In a small bowl, set aside 2 tbsp of the chickpeas.

2 In a food processor, purée the remaining chickpeas with the garlic, water, oil and lemon juice until smooth. During this step, stop the food processor and remove the lid. Using a spatula, scrape down the sides of the food processor. Replace the lid and continue to mix. Season with salt and pepper. The hummus will keep for 5 days in an airtight container in the refrigerator.

3 When ready to serve, transfer the hummus to a shallow serving bowl, making decorative waves on the surface with a spoon. Drizzle with oil, letting it fall between the waves. Top with the reserved chickpeas (see Dip Designer). Sprinkle with the parsley, sesame seeds and paprika. Serve with vegetable crudités or pita bread, if desired.

OG HUMMUS

If you have some tahini (sesame butter), try adding 2 tbsp (30 ml). Traditional hummus always has some in, and it makes your dip super creamy!

Tomato Salsa

63 MILLION

That's about how many kilos of avocados Americans eat during the Super Bowl—the same weight as 12,600 elephants!

Cheesy Avocado Dip

Pita Chips

GOT LEFTOVER PITA BREAD THAT'S A BIT TOO DRY? TURN IT INTO HOMEMADE SPICY CHIPS, THEN THERE'S NO NEED TO RUN TO THE GROCERY STORE!

preparation 15 minutes / **cooking** 12 minutes
makes 32 to 40 chips

2 tbsp	(30 ml) olive oil
1 tsp	chili powder
½ tsp	onion salt
½ tsp	garlic powder
¼ tsp	ground black pepper
4 to 5	medium pita breads

1 With the rack in the middle position, preheat the oven to 350°F (180°C). Line a baking sheet with a silicone mat or parchment paper.

2 In a large bowl, combine the oil with the spices. Set aside.

3 On a work surface, using a chef's knife or kitchen scissors, cut each pita into eight triangles.

4 Add the pita triangles to the bowl of spiced oil. Toss well to coat the pita. Spread the pita out on the baking sheet (the pita triangles will be slightly overlapping).

5 Bake for 12 minutes or until nicely browned, flipping the pita over halfway through cooking.

6 The pita chips will keep for 2 weeks in an airtight container at room temperature.

THEY'RE SOOO GOOD WITH CHEESY AVOCADO DIP (CONVENIENTLY LOCATED ON THE NEXT PAGE) OR HUMMUS (GO BACK FOUR PAGES).

Cheesy Avocado Dip

AN AVOCADO-BASED DIP LIKE GUACAMOLE IS GOOD, BUT ONE WITH ADDED CHEESE IS EVEN BETTER!

preparation 15 minutes / **makes** 2 cups (500 ml)

2	ripe avocados
½ cup	(125 ml) sour cream
2 tbsp	(30 ml) lime juice
3½ oz	(100 g) cheese curds, chopped
1	Lebanese cucumber, cut into small dice
2 tbsp	finely chopped cilantro leaves

1 Using a knife, pierce through the skin and flesh of the avocados until you hit something hard: this is the pit. With the knife, continue cutting all around the pit, keeping the blade straight. Be very careful during this step.

2 Hold one half of the avocado in each hand and turn gently in opposite directions to separate the halves from each other. If the avocado is very ripe, the pit will come out easily. Slide a spoon under the pit and push to remove it. To remove the flesh, slide a spoon between the skin and flesh.

3 In a food processor (see No Food Processor?), purée the avocado flesh with the sour cream and lime juice until smooth. Season with salt and pepper. Transfer to a bowl.

4 Add the cheese curds, cucumber and cilantro to the bowl. Mix well. Season to taste.

5 Serve with pita chips or vegetable crudités. The dip is best enjoyed on the day it is made since the avocado will oxidize and turn brown.

NO FOOD PROCESSOR?

No problem! You can also make this recipe using a bowl and mashing the avocados with a fork. It's a great way to let out some extra energy!

Tomato Salsa

MAKING SALSA IS WAY EASIER THAN DANCING THE SALSA. JUST FOLLOW THESE STEPS: 1-2-3-TOMATO, 1-2-3-PEPPER, 1-2-3-CILANTRO...

preparation 20 minutes / **makes** 1½ cups (375 ml)

4	tomatoes
1	green onion, finely chopped
½	jalapeño chili pepper, seeded and finely chopped (see (Don't) Feel the Burn)
½	lime, juiced
¼ cup	(10 g) finely chopped cilantro leaves

1 On a work surface, using a small knife, remove and compost the stem of the tomatoes. Cut the tomatoes into quarters.

2 Over a bowl, use your thumbs (or a spoon) to push the juice and seeds out of one tomato wedge at a time. Compost the juice and seeds. Wipe out the bowl.

3 Dice the tomatoes. Place in the empty bowl. Add the remaining ingredients. Season with salt and pepper. Mix well.

4 Serve with corn chips. The salsa will keep for 2 days in an airtight container in the refrigerator. Mix well before serving.

(DON'T) FEEL THE BURN!

When seeding peppers, wear food-safe plastic gloves to protect your hands from the burns they can cause. If you don't have gloves, make sure you don't touch your eyes, and wash your hands with soap as soon as you're done handling the peppers.

THE RIGHT TEMPERATURE

The balls will be too soft if left out, so you need to keep them in the fridge or freezer. Always freeze them flat on a baking sheet, because if you put them in a freezer bag first, the soft goodies will get stuck together! Once they're frozen, move them to an airtight container and continue storing them in the freezer.

Energy Balls

FEELING A BIT FLAT? RECHARGE YOUR BATTERIES WITH THESE ROUND CHOCOLATE TREATS!

preparation 50 minutes / **chilling** 3 hours
makes about 3 dozen / **freezes well**

BALLS

¾ cup	(135 g) Medjool dates, pitted
⅓ cup	(35 g) cocoa powder
½ cup	(125 ml) water
⅓ cup	(75 ml) almond butter
¼ cup	(60 ml) maple syrup
1 tsp	(5 ml) vanilla
½ tsp	ground cinnamon
2 cups	(280 g) graham cracker crumbs

TOPPINGS

	Multicolored candy sprinkles
	Sesame seeds, lightly roasted
	Coconut flakes
	Unsalted shelled pistachios, lightly roasted and chopped

BALLS

1 In a food processor, purée the dates with the cocoa powder, water, almond butter, maple syrup, vanilla and cinnamon until smooth.

2 Add the graham crumbs to the food processor and blend until smooth. During this step, stop the food processor and remove the lid. Using a spatula, scrape down the sides of the food processor. Replace the lid and continue to mix.

3 Transfer the mixture to a bowl. Cover and refrigerate for 2 hours, until firm.

4 Using a 1 tbsp (15 ml) ice cream scoop, shape the mixture into balls. Finish rolling the balls with your hands. Place the balls evenly spaced out on a baking sheet lined with parchment paper.

TOPPINGS

5 Place the toppings of your choice in shallow dishes.

6 Roll a few balls at a time in the toppings, pressing lightly to coat well. Return the balls to the baking sheet. Refrigerate for 1 hour before serving, or freeze.

7 The energy balls will keep for 3 weeks in an airtight container in the refrigerator or for 3 months in the freezer.

CLEAN HANDS

After you've shaped a few balls, make sure to wash your hands again. This way, it'll be easier to keep rolling the rest!

Applesauce

APPLESAUCE DOESN'T HAVE TO BE COMPLICATED! APPLES AND WATER ARE ALL YOU NEED TO COOK YOUR U-PICK HAUL. DON'T WORRY: GROCERY STORE APPLES WORK, TOO!

- -

preparation 20 minutes / **cooking** 15 minutes
chilling 2 hours / **makes** 2 cups (500 ml)
freezes well

½ cup	(125 ml) water
4 cups	(440 g) McIntosh apples, unpeeled, cored and cubed (about 4 medium apples)

1 Place the water and apples in a pot. Bring to a boil. Simmer for 10 minutes or until the apples have softened.

2 In a blender or food processor, purée the apple mixture until smooth. Watch out for splattering.

3 Transfer the applesauce to an airtight container and let cool. Cover and refrigerate for 2 hours or until completely chilled. The applesauce will keep for 5 days in the refrigerator.

LIKE IT SWEET?
For an applesauce that tastes like dessert, add ¼ cup (55 g) sugar to the apples as they cook.

If you blend the cooked apples in a food processor, your arm muscles won't turn to mush!

APPLE PEEL
=
PINK APPLESAUCE

Oatmeal Cookies with Three Toppings

WITH JUST ONE OATMEAL COOKIE RECIPE, YOU CAN HAVE THREE TIMES THE FUN! CHOOSE YOUR MIX-INS BASED ON YOUR MOOD.

preparation 25 minutes / **cooking** 16 minutes per batch
cooling 1 hour per batch / **makes** 1 dozen / **freezes well**

1¾ cups	(175 g) quick cook oats	
¾ cup	(115 g) unbleached all-purpose flour	
½ tsp	baking soda	
¼ tsp	salt	
½ cup	(115 g) unsalted butter, softened	
1 cup	(210 g) brown sugar	
½ tsp	(2.5 ml) vanilla	
1	egg	
1 tbsp	(15 ml) milk	
	Topping of your choice (see next page)	

1 With the rack in the middle position, preheat the oven to 350°F (180°C). Line two baking sheets with silicone mats or parchment paper.

2 In a bowl, combine the oats, flour, baking soda and salt.

3 In another bowl, cream the butter, brown sugar and vanilla with an electric mixer on low speed for 2 minutes. Add the egg and mix until smooth. With the machine or using a wooden spoon, stir in the dry ingredients and milk. Mix to combine.

4 Using a 3 tbsp (45 ml) ice cream scoop, shape the mixture into balls, placing six on each baking sheet. Flatten the balls slightly with a fork or with your hand. Garnish each cookie with 1 tbsp of the topping of your choice (see next page) or leave plain.

5 Bake one sheet at a time for 16 minutes or until the cookies are golden. Remove from the oven and let cool completely on a wire rack, about 1 hour.

6 The cookies will keep for 3 days in an airtight container at room temperature.

PEANUT + TOFFEE

CHOCOLATE + CRANBERRY

APPLE + RAISIN

FOLLOW HERE FOR THE MIX-INS

COOKIE CREATIONS

Check out these three ingredient combos you can add to your oatmeal cookie dough before baking. For endless snack ideas, mix in fresh or dried fruit, nuts and toffee or chocolate chips. Get creative and have fun with your cookies!

PEANUT & TOFFEE

In a small bowl, combine 6 tbsp (60 g) roasted unsalted peanuts with 6 tbsp (60 g) English toffee bits (see Small Bits).

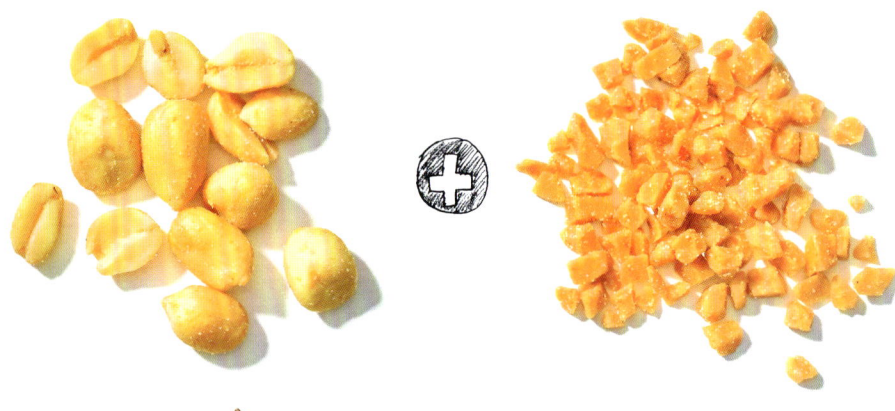

CHOCOLATE & CRANBERRY

In a small bowl, combine 6 tbsp (60 g) chopped dark chocolate with 6 tbsp (60 g) dried cranberries.

APPLE & RAISIN

In a glass bowl, combine 1 small Cortland apple, unpeeled, cored and diced, with 1 tbsp (13 g) sugar. Cover with plastic wrap. Cook in the microwave for 2 minutes or until the apple is soft but firm. Add 3 tbsp (25 g) raisins and combine. Let cool while you prepare the cookie dough. Drain before garnishing your cookies.

SMALL BITS
You can find English toffee bits in most supermarkets in the baking aisle, usually right next to the chocolate chips.

CHEWY BANANA-
SESAME GRANOLA BARS

CHEWY PEANUT-
CRANBERRY GRANOLA BARS

Chewy Banana-Sesame Granola Bars

SINCE THEY'RE NUT-FREE, THESE CHEWY BARS MADE WITH PURÉED DATES ARE THE PERFECT SNACK TO TAKE TO SCHOOL.

preparation 30 minutes / **cooking** 30 minutes
cooling 3 hours / **makes** 16 / **freezes well**

1 cup	(170 g) pitted and chopped Medjool dates
3 tbsp	unsalted butter
¼ cup	(60 ml) water
¼ cup	(60 ml) honey
¼ cup	(60 ml) tahini
1½ cups	(150 g) quick cook oats
1 cup	(25 g) puffed rice cereal
¾ cup	(70 g) dried banana slices, crushed
½ cup	(45 g) unsweetened shredded or grated coconut
¼ cup	(35 g) roasted sesame seeds
¼ tsp	salt
3 oz	(85 g) dark chocolate, coarsely chopped

1 With the rack in the middle position, preheat the oven to 325°F (165°C). Butter a 13 × 9-inch (33 × 23 cm) rectangular pan and line with a strip of parchment paper, letting it hang over two sides, to help with unmolding.

2 In a small pot over medium heat, bring the dates, butter, water, honey and tahini to a boil. Simmer for 5 minutes, stirring constantly with a wooden spoon, until the dates have reduced to a purée. Remove from the heat and let cool.

3 In a bowl, combine the remaining ingredients except for the chocolate. Add the date purée. Mix well with a spatula to coat the dry ingredients. Stir in the chocolate. Spread the mixture out in the prepared pan in an even layer. To help with this step, cover the mixture with a piece of parchment paper and press down with a rolling pin or a flat object. Remove this top piece of parchment paper.

4 Bake for 20 minutes or until the sides start to brown. Remove from the oven and let cool completely on a wire rack, about 3 hours.

5 Unmold onto a work surface, and cut into 16 bars. The granola bars will keep for 1 week in an airtight container at room temperature. They will get softer after a few days.

NUT-FREE

Q&A TIME WITH QUENTIN

SO WHAT IS **TAHINI** ANYWAY?
It's a sesame butter made from untoasted sesame seeds. It tastes a bit like peanut butter and works great in sauces.

Chewy Peanut-Cranberry Granola Bars

YOU DON'T NEED AN OVEN FOR THESE CHEWY BARS—JUST A STOVE FOR A QUICK COOK. HEAT A FEW INGREDIENTS, COMBINE EVERYTHING TOGETHER, AND LET THE BARS SET IN THE FRIDGE.

preparation 25 minutes / **cooking** 5 minutes
chilling 1 hour / **makes** 16

1½ cups	(150 g)	quick cook oats
1½ cups	(40 g)	puffed rice cereal
¾ cup	(80 g)	milk powder
¼ cup	(40 g)	unsalted roasted peanuts
¼ cup	(40 g)	roasted pumpkin seeds
¼ cup	(40 g)	dried cranberries or raisins
⅔ cup	(150 ml)	clear corn syrup
½ cup	(125 ml)	creamy peanut butter
2 tbsp		sugar
2 tbsp	(30 ml)	vegetable oil

1 Lightly oil an 8-inch (20 cm) square pan and line with plastic wrap, letting it hang over all four sides, to help with unmolding.

2 In a large bowl, combine the oats, rice cereal, milk powder, peanuts, pumpkin seeds and cranberries.

3 In a small pot over medium heat, bring the corn syrup, peanut butter, sugar and oil to a boil while whisking. Pour over the oat mixture in the large bowl and mix well with a wooden spoon to coat the dry ingredients. Finish mixing with lightly oiled hands to make sure the ingredients stick together well. Spread the mixture out in the prepared pan.

4 Place a square of parchment paper or plastic wrap over the mixture and press firmly into an even layer with your hands. Refrigerate for 1 hour.

5 Unmold onto a work surface and remove the plastic wrap. Cut into 16 bars. The granola bars will keep for 3 weeks in an airtight container at room temperature.

NO OVEN REQUIRED

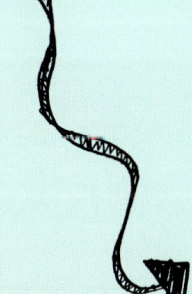

CHEWY BAR CEMENT

Milk powder and peanut butter help hold the cereal together. Corn syrup also helps bind everything, but it's less sweet than honey or maple syrup, so don't swap it out. These chewy bars will keep firming up a few hours after coming out of the fridge.

SMART TIP

If you oil the baking dish, the plastic wrap will stay put when you press in the mixture of ingredients.

WHO ATE MY MUFFIN?

Banana Muffins

AT THE SCHOOL OF MUFFINS, THE BANANA MUFFIN IS ALWAYS AT THE TOP OF THE CLASS. IT'S SO TENDER AND SOFT, IT GETS AN A+ EACH AND EVERY TIME!

preparation 20 minutes / **cooking** 22 minutes
cooling 1 hour / **makes** 1 dozen / **freezes well**

1½ cups	(225 g) whole wheat flour
1 tsp	baking powder
1 tsp	ground cinnamon
½ tsp	baking soda
¼ tsp	salt
3	very ripe bananas
½ cup	(105 g) brown sugar
2	eggs
⅓ cup	(75 ml) vegetable oil
¼ cup	(60 ml) milk

1 With the rack in the middle position, preheat the oven to 350°F (180°C). Line a 12-cup muffin pan with silicone or paper liners.

2 In a bowl, combine the flour, baking powder, cinnamon, baking soda and salt.

3 In another bowl, coarsely mash the bananas with a fork. Add the brown sugar, eggs, oil and milk. Whisk until smooth. Using a spatula, gently stir in the dry ingredients until just moistened. Divide the batter among the muffin cups.

4 Bake for 22 to 25 minutes or until a toothpick inserted in the center of the muffins comes out clean. Remove from the oven and let cool completely on a wire rack, about 1 hour, before unmolding.

5 The muffins will keep for 3 days in an airtight container at room temperature.

HOORAY FOR BROWN BANANAS!

The best bananas for muffins are the ones with black spots that have started to turn brown. They're sweeter and easier to mash! You can also keep brown bananas in the freezer for up to 3 months if you want to use them later.

ECO-FRIENDLY TINS

Silicone molds are handy for easily removing muffins, and the best part is you can use them over and over again!

Yogurt-Raspberry Cookies

THESE COOKIES HAVE THE SAME TEXTURE AS MUFFIN TOPS. FINALLY, YOU CAN JUST HAVE THE BEST PART OF THE MUFFIN!

preparation 20 minutes / **cooking** 10 minutes per batch
cooling 1 hour per batch / **makes** 16 / **freezes well**

1 cup	(150 g) unbleached all-purpose flour
½ tsp	baking soda
¼ tsp	salt
⅓ cup	(70 g) brown sugar
2 tbsp	butter, melted
2	eggs
¼ cup	(60 ml) 2% plain Greek yogurt
3 oz	(85 g) white chocolate, coarsely chopped
½ cup	(70 g) fresh raspberries
½ cup	(65 g) unsalted shelled pistachios, chopped

1 With the rack in the middle position, preheat the oven to 350°F (180°C). Line two baking sheets with silicone mats or parchment paper.

2 In a bowl, combine the flour, baking soda and salt.

3 In another bowl, combine the brown sugar and melted butter with an electric mixer on low speed for 2 minutes. Add the eggs one at a time until smooth. With the machine running, stir in the yogurt and flour mixture. Add the chocolate, raspberries and pistachios. Mix gently with a spatula just until the mixture is moistened.

4 Using a 2 tbsp (30 ml) ice cream scoop, place eight balls of the mixture on each baking sheet, evenly spacing them out.

5 Bake one sheet at a time for 10 to 12 minutes or until the cookies are golden around the edges but still very soft at the center. Remove from the oven and let cool completely on the baking sheets, about 1 hour.

6 The cookies will keep for 3 days in an airtight container at room temperature.

I WANT RASPBERRY YOGURT

I WANT COOKIES

Fruit Salad

MUSHY BANANAS AND KIWI? NO, THANKS!
FOR THIS SALAD, CHOOSE FRUITS THAT WILL
STAY FIRM FOR DAYS.

preparation 25 minutes / **cooking** 5 minutes
chilling 3 hours / **servings** 10

SYRUP
1½ cups	(375 ml) water
6 tbsp	(80 g) sugar
1	orange, zest and juice

SALAD
1	pineapple, peeled, cored and cut into large dice
1	small cantaloupe, peeled, seeded and cut into large dice
2	sweet, crisp red apples (such as Pink Lady, Honeycrisp, Royal Gala), unpeeled, cored and cut into large dice
1 tbsp	(15 ml) lemon juice
1¼ cups	(190 g) fresh blueberries

SYRUP

1 In a small pot, bring the water, sugar, orange zest and orange juice to a boil just until the sugar has dissolved.

2 Strain the syrup through a sieve set over a large measuring cup or bowl. Compost the zest. Let the syrup cool.

SALAD

3 Meanwhile, place the diced pineapple, cantaloupe and apples in a large 8-cup (2 L) bowl. Add the cooled syrup, lemon juice and blueberries. Mix gently. Cover and let marinate in the refrigerator for 3 hours or until the salad is chilled.

4 The fruit salad will keep for 4 days in an airtight container in the refrigerator.

GROW YOUR OWN PINEAPPLE

To do this, slice off the crown of the pineapple at the part where the leaves meet the fruit. Plant it in a jar filled with 4 to 6 inches (10 to 15 cm) of moist soil. Roots will begin to form in 1 to 3 months, and new leaves will begin to grow, making for a rather pretty plant. As for the pineapple, you'll have to be patient; the fruit will grow in about 4 or 5 years!

CHAPTER 03

SO...WHAT ARE WE EATING?!

IT'S NOW YOUR TURN TO ANSWER THIS QUESTION! YOU GET TO DECIDE WHAT YOU WANT TO EAT FOR LUNCH AND DINNER. OK, MAYBE NOT CHOCOLATE CHIP COOKIES, BUT YOU CAN CHOOSE FROM THIS CHAPTER OF YOUR NEW FAVORITE MEALS!

YES! we're STARTING with PASTA!

Chicken Fettuccine Alfredo

PRACTICE YOUR ITALIAN BY SAYING WORDS LIKE "ALFREDO," "PARMIGIANO REGGIANO" AND A BUNCH OF OTHER WORDS THAT END WITH "O"! BUON APPETITO—THAT'S HOW YOU CAN TELL SOMEONE TO ENJOY THEIR MEAL IN ITALIAN!

preparation 20 minutes / **cooking** 25 minutes / **servings** 4

¾ lb	(340 g) fettuccine
3	boneless, skinless chicken breasts
¼ cup	(55 g) butter
1	garlic clove, finely chopped
¾ cup	(180 ml) 35% cream
¾ cup	(55 g) grated fresh Parmesan cheese

1 In a large pot of salted boiling water, cook the pasta until al dente (see Al Dente p. 69). Set aside ½ cup (125 ml) of the cooking water. Drain the pasta and lightly oil.

2 Meanwhile, on a work surface, cut the chicken in half horizontally to get two thin cutlets per breast. Slice each cutlet into strips.

3 In a large non-stick skillet over high heat, brown the chicken in half of the butter (2 tbsp). Season with salt and pepper. Add the garlic and cook for 1 minute while stirring. Set aside on a plate.

4 In the same pot used to cook the pasta, bring the 35% cream, cheese and remaining butter to a boil while whisking. Over medium heat, add the cooked pasta, chicken and ¼ cup (60 ml) of the reserved pasta cooking water. Reheat the pasta while stirring with kitchen tongs until the liquid is absorbed. Add more pasta cooking water as needed to thin out the sauce or if the pasta is too sticky. Season to taste.

5 Divide the pasta among four shallow bowls and serve immediately.

Q&A TIME WITH QUENTIN

WHO EXACTLY IS ALFREDO?

Chef Alfredo Di Lelio created this yummy dish at his restaurant in Rome, Italy, in the early 1900s. It was so delicious that the recipe traveled all the way here (and by here, we mean this page)!

AL DENTE

Cooking pasta "al dente" means cooking it only until it's firm to the bite—not soft or mushy. On pasta boxes, the cooking time provided is usually for al dente pasta.

{ YOUR GUIDE TO PASTA }

MACARONI, SPAGHETTI, ROTINI... FEELING DIZZY TRYING TO REMEMBER ALL THE PASTA NAMES? HERE ARE SOME IMPORTANT NOODLES YOU SHOULD KNOW SO YOU CAN MAKE LOTS OF DIFFERENT RECIPES (OR AT LEAST THE ONES IN THIS BOOK).

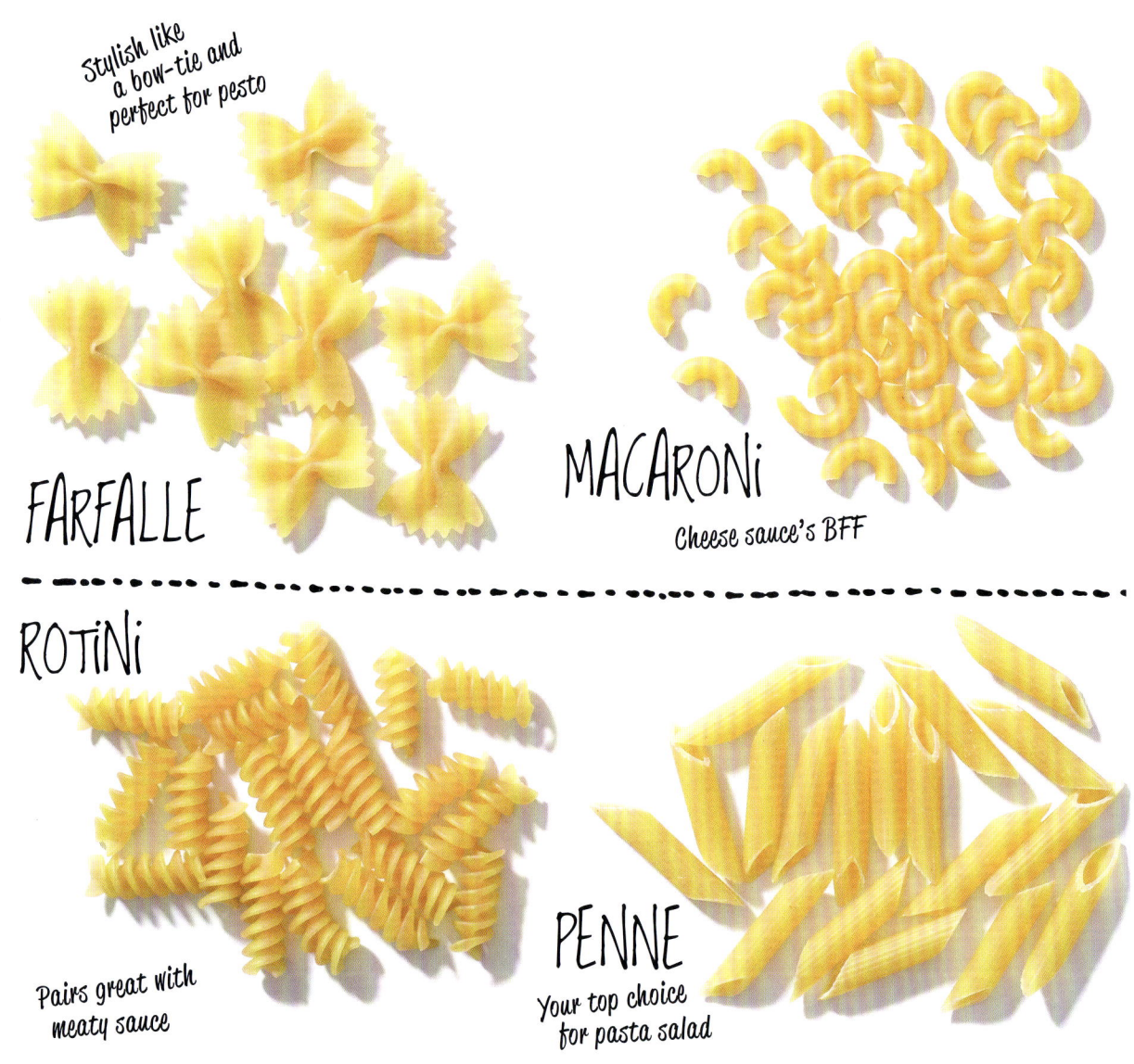

SHORT PASTA

Stylish like a bow-tie and perfect for pesto

FARFALLE

MACARONI

Cheese sauce's BFF

ROTINI

Pairs great with meaty sauce

PENNE

Your top choice for pasta salad

LONG PASTA

SPAGHETTI
A classic to go with
classic tomato sauce

RAMEN
Not really a pasta, but these
squiggly noodles for recipes with Asian flavors

LINGUINE
A great choice
with seafood

FETTUCCINE
Flat pasta soaks up
even more sauce!

GIANT
MEATBALL

VS

MINI
MEATBALLS

ONE GIANT MEATBALL = 12 MINI MEATBALLS

(DON'T) GO BIG

You can make mini meatballs with this recipe instead.

1. Preheat the oven to broil.
2. Using a 1 tbsp (15 ml) ice cream scoop, shape the meat mixture into about 48 small balls. Finish rolling them into meatballs with lightly oiled hands.
3. Place the mini meatballs on the baking sheet.
4. Broil for 10 minutes, turning them over halfway through cooking.

Broccoli Meatballs

WHETHER YOU ROLL BIG OR SMALL MEATBALLS, THEY'LL BE SOFT AND TASTY THANKS TO BREADCRUMBS...AND BROCCOLI!

preparation 25 minutes / **cooking** 30 minutes / **servings** 4
freezes well

½ cup	(40 g) panko breadcrumbs
3 tbsp	(45 ml) milk
2 cups	(160 g) small broccoli florets (see Veggie Swap)
1 lb	(450 g) mixed ground meat (veal, beef and pork) (or choose just 1 type of meat)
1	egg
1	garlic clove, finely chopped

1 With the rack in the middle position, preheat the oven to 450°F (230°C). Line a baking sheet with foil. Lightly oil the foil.

2 In a large bowl, combine the breadcrumbs and milk. Let soak for 5 minutes.

3 In a food processor, finely chop the broccoli. Transfer to the bowl of breadcrumbs. Add the remaining ingredients to the bowl. Season with salt and pepper. Mix with your hands.

4 With lightly oiled hands, shape the mixture into four large meatballs and place on the baking sheet (see (Don't) Go Big for mini meatballs). Bake for 30 to 35 minutes or until the meatballs are cooked through and golden. Serve with spaghetti and tomato sauce, if desired.

VEGGIE SWAP

You can replace broccoli with a large carrot. Just peel and dice it, then chop it up in a food processor. If you don't have a food processor, you can use a grater to shred your vegetables.

Basic Tomato Sauce

YOU ONLY NEED FOUR INGREDIENTS TO MAKE THIS CLASSIC SAUCE THAT GOES GREAT WITH ANY PASTA SHAPE. IT'S SO EASY!

preparation 15 minutes / **cooking** 40 minutes
makes about 3 cups (750 ml) / **freezes well**

1 can	(28 oz/796 ml) whole plum tomatoes
1	onion, finely chopped
1	garlic clove, finely chopped
2 tbsp	(30 ml) olive oil

1 In a bowl, crush the tomatoes with clean hands.

2 In a pot over medium heat, cook the onion and garlic in the oil without letting them brown (see Spice Up Your Sauce). Season with salt and pepper.

3 Add the tomatoes to the pot and mix well. Bring to a boil. Simmer gently over very low heat for 30 minutes. Watch out for splattering. Season to taste.

NO MORE STAINS

Don't forget to wear an apron to protect your new shirt from tomato splatter!

SPICE UP YOUR SAUCE

For a spicier version, add ¼ tsp (1 ml) red pepper flakes.

PERFECTO!

To figure out how much long pasta to cook for each person, you can make the "OK" hand gesture by putting your thumb and index finger together. The amount you can hold in the circle you've made is a good portion for one person, but since your fingers and your parents' fingers are different sizes, you can use the circle below to be even more precise!

I love you a little, a lot, madly...

Pasta with Rosé Sauce

MAYBE IT'S THE PRETTY PINK COLOR, LIKE VALENTINE'S DAY, THAT MAKES EVERYONE LOVE THIS SAUCE!

----

preparation 30 minutes / **cooking** 25 minutes / **servings** 4

TOMATO SAUCE
1	onion, chopped
2	garlic cloves, finely chopped
2 tbsp	(30 ml) olive oil
1 can	(28 oz/796 ml) crushed or whole plum tomatoes
3 tbsp	(45 ml) tomato paste

BÉCHAMEL SAUCE (see 1 Sauce, 2 Ways)
2 tbsp	butter
2 tbsp	unbleached all-purpose flour
1 cup	(250 ml) milk
¾ lb	(340 g) long or short pasta of your choice

TOMATO SAUCE

1 In a pot over medium heat, soften the onion and garlic in the oil for 3 minutes. Add the tomatoes and tomato paste. Mix well and bring to a boil. Simmer for 15 minutes, stirring often. Watch out for splattering. Season with salt and pepper.

2 In a blender, purée the sauce until smooth. Return to the pot and keep warm.

BÉCHAMEL SAUCE

3 Meanwhile, in a small pot over medium heat, melt the butter. Add the flour and cook for 1 minute while stirring with a whisk. Pour in the milk. Bring to a boil while whisking constantly. Simmer for 3 minutes. Season with salt and pepper.

4 Pour the béchamel into the pot of tomato sauce. Mix well. Season to taste.

5 Meanwhile, in a large pot of salted boiling water, cook the pasta until al dente (see Al Dente p. 69). Drain the pasta. Add the pasta to the pot of sauce and mix to coat well.

6 Divide the pasta among four shallow bowls and serve immediately.

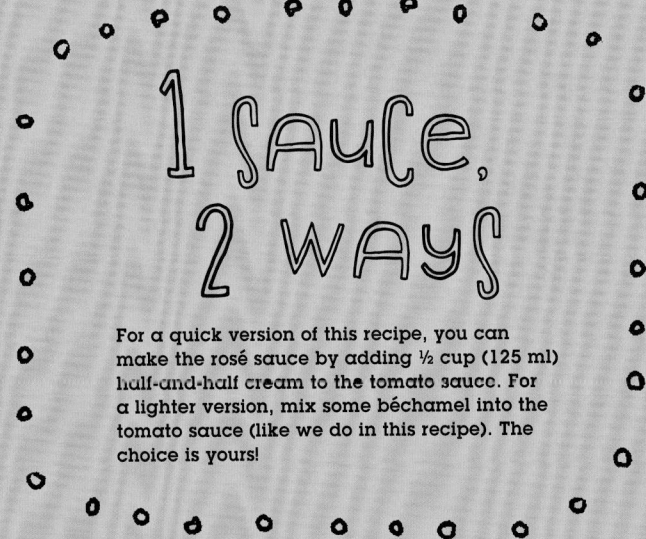

1 Sauce, 2 Ways

For a quick version of this recipe, you can make the rosé sauce by adding ½ cup (125 ml) half-and-half cream to the tomato sauce. For a lighter version, mix some béchamel into the tomato sauce (like we do in this recipe). The choice is yours!

CAESAR SALAD

LETTUCE TALK CAESAR-ISHLY!

No, Julius Caesar did not eat this salad during the Roman Empire! (He also didn't invent it.) It was actually in the 1920s that Italian chef Cesare Cardini, who was living in the United States, invented the salad in a restaurant...in Mexico! 100 years later, it's one of the most popular salads in North America.

GREEK
SALAD

CAESAR SALAD

LIKE A ROMAN EMPEROR, TAKE CHARGE OF DINNER! TRY THIS CAESAR SALAD WITH CREAMY DRESSING, PARMESAN AND BACON—YUM!

- -

preparation 25 minutes / **cooking** 5 minutes / **servings** 4

DRESSING

⅓ cup	(75 ml) mayonnaise
¼ cup	(20 g) finely grated fresh Parmesan cheese
2 tbsp	(30 ml) lemon juice
1 tbsp	(15 ml) Dijon mustard
1 tbsp	capers, chopped
1	garlic clove, finely grated

SALAD

2 cups	(100 g) cubed bread
2 tbsp	(30 ml) olive oil
2	romaine lettuce hearts, leaves torn
8	slices cooked bacon, chopped (recipe p. 83)
	Fresh Parmesan cheese, coarsely grated, for serving

DRESSING

1 In a salad bowl or large bowl, whisk together all of the ingredients. Season generously with pepper.

SALAD

2 In a skillet over medium-high heat, brown the bread in the oil for 5 minutes. Season lightly with salt and pepper. Remove from the heat. You now have homemade croutons.

3 Add the lettuce, bacon and croutons to the bowl of dressing. Mix well. Season to taste.

4 Divide the salad among four plates. Garnish with Parmesan. Serve immediately.

GREEK SALAD

NEXT STOP: GREECE! BUCKLE UP FOR A TASTY ADVENTURE. THANK YOU FOR FLYING WITH AIR RICARDO.

preparation 30 minutes / **servings** 4

DRESSING

3 tbsp	(45 ml) olive oil
2 tbsp	(30 ml) lemon juice
2 tbsp	pitted and finely chopped kalamata olives
2 tbsp	finely chopped flat-leaf parsley
1 tsp	sugar
1 tsp	(5 ml) Dijon mustard
½ tsp	dried oregano

SALAD

4	tomatoes, cubed
1	English cucumber, cubed
1	yellow bell pepper, seeded and cubed
1	small red onion, thinly sliced (see Onions Can Be Stinky!)
3 oz	(85 g) feta cheese, diced

NOW BOARDING

DRESSING

1 In a salad bowl or large bowl, whisk together all of the ingredients.

SALAD

2 Add all of the salad ingredients to the bowl of dressing. Season with salt and pepper. Mix well.

3 Serve immediately, or cover and refrigerate until ready to serve.

ONIONS CAN BE STINKY!

To keep the smell of onions from scaring off your friends (and to save your breath), soak chopped onions in cold water for 10 minutes, then drain them before adding to your salad.

PERFECTLY GOLDEN
Want crispy bread? You can use a toaster or bake your bread slices in the oven. Just pop them on a baking sheet and let them brown for 2 minutes on each side.

BLT Sandwiches

WHILE LOTS OF SANDWICH FILLINGS ARE YUMMY, THERE'S JUST NOTHING QUITE LIKE THE COMBINATION OF BACON, LETTUCE AND TOMATO.

preparation 15 minutes / **servings** 2

4	slices bread, toasted (see Perfectly Golden p. 82)
¼ cup	(60 ml) mayonnaise
2	leaves curly-leaf or Boston lettuce
4	slices tomato
4	slices cooked bacon
OR	
½	recipe tofu bacon

1 Spread the bread slices with the mayonnaise. Divide the lettuce, tomatoes and bacon between two slices of bread. Season with salt and pepper.

2 Top the sandwiches with the remaining bread slices. Cut in half and serve immediately.

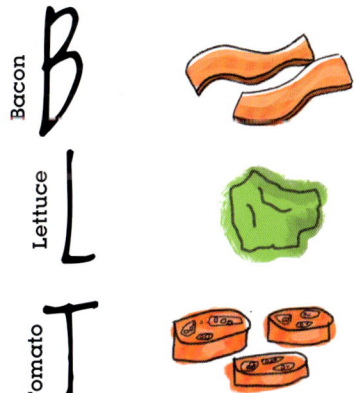

Cooked Bacon

preparation 5 minutes / **cooking** 15 minutes / **servings** 4

4	slices bacon

1 With the rack in the middle position, preheat the oven to 400°F (200°C). Line a baking sheet with a silicone mat or parchment paper.

2 Place the bacon on the baking sheet. Bake for 15 minutes or until crispy. Once out of the oven, drain on a plate lined with paper towels.

3 The cooked bacon will keep for 2 weeks in an airtight container in the refrigerator.

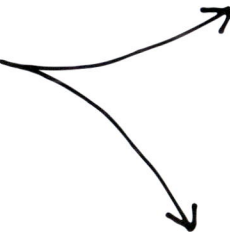

Tofu Bacon

preparation 15 minutes / **cooking** 20 minutes / **servings** 4

2 tbsp	(30 ml) low-sodium soy sauce
2 tbsp	(30 ml) vegetable oil
1 tbsp	brown sugar
1½ tsp	smoked paprika
1 tsp	onion powder
¾ lb	(340 g) extra-firm tofu, cut lengthwise into slices ⅛ inch (3 mm) thick

1 With the rack in the middle position, preheat the oven to 375°F (190°C). Line a baking sheet with a silicone mat or parchment paper.

2 In a bowl, whisk together the soy sauce, oil, brown sugar and spices. Dip the tofu slices in the marinade one at a time and place on the baking sheet. Set the marinade aside.

3 Bake for 15 minutes. Remove the baking sheet from the oven. Using a pastry brush, cover the tofu slices with the reserved marinade. Continue to bake for 5 minutes or until the sides of the tofu slices are golden.

4 The tofu bacon will keep for 1 week in an airtight container in the refrigerator.

GEOMETRY LESSON

Totally non-scientific studies say grilled cheese sandwiches taste best when cut into triangles!

The Best Grilled Cheese

GOOEY ORANGE CHEESE BETWEEN TWO SLICES OF BREAD IS ALL IT TAKES TO MAKE A COZY LUNCH. IF IT AIN'T BROKE, DON'T FIX IT!

preparation 5 minutes / **cooking** 6 minutes / **serving** 1

1 tbsp	butter, softened
2	slices white bread
2	slices orange cheddar cheese

1 On a work surface, butter one side of each bread slice (see You'll Thank Us Later p. 85). Place the cheese on the unbuttered side of one bread slice. Close the sandwich with the remaining bread slice, butter-side up.

2 In a non-stick skillet over medium heat, cook the sandwich on one side for 3 minutes or until golden. Using a spatula, flip the sandwich over and press down lightly to flatten. Continue to cook until golden on the second side and the cheese has melted.

3 Let the grilled cheese rest for 2 minutes. Cut in half and serve with vegetable crudités, if desired.

YOU'LL THANK US
LATER
⬇

For an even creamier texture, spread some mayonnaise on the inside of the bread before grilling.

STRETCH YOUR LIMITS

FOR THE CHEESIEST AND GOOIEST GRILLED CHEESE SANDWICH OR MAC AND CHEESE, CHOOSE STRETCHY, MELTY CHEESES.

MOZZARELLA

CHEDDAR

MONTEREY JACK

GRUYÈRE

SWISS PROVOLONE

GOUDA

IN A SKILLET?

It's true! You don't need a fancy wood-burning oven for pizza night! Just coat your skillet and pizza dough with oil so they don't stick. Make sure your skillet can go in the oven—check the bottom for a small symbol or ask a grown-up.

Skillet Pizza

WITH THIS SUPER EASY RECIPE, YOU'LL BE MAKING PIZZAS JUST AS GOOD AS THE LOCAL PIZZA SPOT—OR MAYBE EVEN BETTER! YOU MIGHT EVEN START YOUR OWN DELIVERY SERVICE!

preparation 15 minutes / **cooking** 20 minutes / **servings** 4

1	recipe Pizza Dough, risen in a skillet (p. 90)
½	recipe No-Cook Tomato Sauce (recipe opposite)
½ cup	(90 g) small, thin slices salami
1 cup	(100 g) grated mozzarella cheese
¼	red bell pepper, seeded and cut into small dice
¼	green bell pepper, seeded and cut into small dice

1 With the rack in the middle position, preheat the oven to 400°F (200°C).

2 With your fingertips, press the middle of the pizza dough so that the center is flat but the edge remains puffy all the way around.

3 Using a spoon, spread the tomato sauce over the center of the dough only, avoiding the edge. Top with half of the salami slices. Cover the sauce and salami with the cheese. Add the bell peppers and remaining salami.

4 Bake for 20 minutes or until the dough is golden and the cheese has melted.

5 Slide the pizza from the skillet onto a cutting board. Cut into wedges and serve.

FOLLOW TO MAKE YOUR
PIZZA DOUGH

No-Cook Tomato Sauce

IMPRESS ADULTS BY TELLING THEM YOU NEED WHOLE ITALIAN TOMATOES, NOT DICED ONES. WHOLE TOMATOES WILL MAKE YOUR SAUCE TASTE WAY BETTER!

preparation 15 minutes / **makes about** 1½ cups (375 ml)

1 can	(28 oz/796 ml) whole plum tomatoes
2	garlic cloves, finely chopped
2 tbsp	(30 ml) olive oil
1 tbsp	(15 ml) tomato paste
¼ tsp	red pepper flakes (optional)

1 Strain the tomatoes through a sieve placed over a bowl. Save the tomato juice for another use (for example: soup). Wipe out the bowl.

2 Over the clean bowl, remove the seeds and excess natural juices from the center of each tomato (see No More Soggy Crusts). Compost the juice and seeds. Wipe out the bowl again.

3 In the empty bowl, coarsely crush the tomatoes with clean hands. Add the remaining ingredients. Season with salt and pepper. Mix well with a wooden spoon.

4 The tomato sauce will keep for 3 days in an airtight container in the refrigerator.

This recipe makes enough sauce for two pizzas.

NO MORE SOGGY CRUSTS
By removing the seeds from tomatoes, you're getting rid of the extra moisture. Your sauce will be thicker and won't make your pizza dough soggy.

Pizza Dough

WITH THE RIGHT TECHNIQUE, IT REALLY ISN'T THAT HARD TO MAKE. YOU'LL SEE!

preparation 15 minutes / **rising** 1 h 30
makes enough for 1 skillet pizza

1 cup	+ 2 tbsp (170 g) unbleached all-purpose flour
1 tsp	sugar
1 tsp	instant yeast
½ tsp	salt
½ cup	(125 ml) warm water
3 tbsp	(45 ml) vegetable oil

1 In a large bowl, using a wooden spoon, combine the flour, sugar, yeast and salt. Add the water and mix just until the dough starts to form into a ball.

2 On a floured work surface, knead the dough for 5 minutes or until smooth. Add a little more flour if the dough is sticky.

3 Using a rolling pin, roll the dough out to form a 10-inch (25 cm) circle.

4 Spread half of the oil out in a large 11-inch (28 cm) skillet or round baking dish. Place the dough in the oiled skillet. Using a pastry brush, cover the surface of the dough with the remaining oil. Cover with plastic wrap and let rise in a warm, humid spot for 1 hour 30 minutes or until the dough has doubled in volume.

GET ROLLIN'
Roll out your dough with a rolling pin. It's way easier than trying to toss it in the air like a pro! (Plus, you won't end up with dough on your head.)

MY FIRST PIZZA!

GOT A SWEET TOOTH?
This is the same dough used in our Chocolate-Banana Dessert Pizza (p. 188).

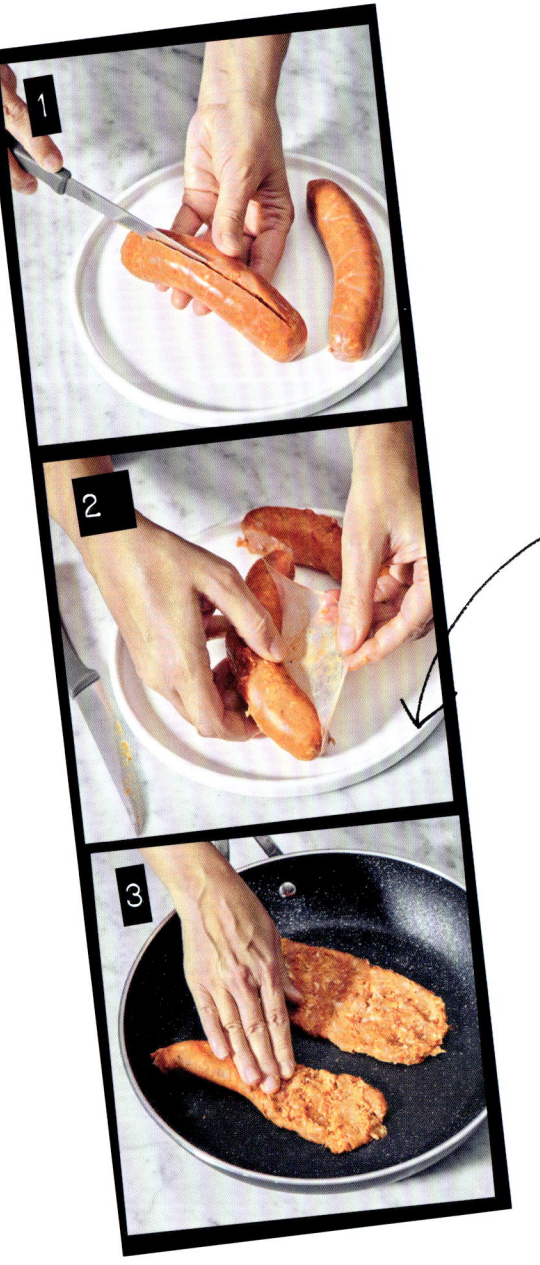

Smashed Sausage Subs

EVER HAD A SMASHED SANDWICH? YOU WILL HAVE AFTER THIS! CRUSH YOUR SAUSAGE MEAT BEFORE ADDING IT TO YOUR SUB AND TASTE THE DIFFERENCE!

preparation 15 minutes / **cooking** 10 minutes / **servings** 2

2	submarine buns, each 7 inches (18 cm) long
2	mild or spicy Italian sausages, casings removed
1 cup	(100 g) grated mozzarella cheese
4	slices tomato, halved
	Iceberg lettuce, thinly sliced, to taste
	Store-bought French dressing, to taste

1 With the rack in the middle position, preheat the oven to 400°F (200°C).

2 On a work surface, cut the buns in half horizontally without going all the way through to the other side. Open them like a book and place face-up on a non-stick or parchment paper–lined baking sheet.

3 In a large non-stick skillet, off the heat, place the sausage meat. Using your hands, press the meat into two thin patties the same length as the buns.

4 Cook the sausage patties over medium heat for 5 minutes or until golden. Flip them over and sprinkle with the cheese. Continue to cook on the second side until the cheese has melted.

5 Meanwhile, toast the buns in the oven for 5 minutes. Remove from the oven.

6 Fill the warm buns with the cheesy sausage patties. Top with the tomato slices and lettuce. Drizzle with French dressing.

HOW TO REMOVE SAUSAGE MEAT FROM THE CASING

1 Using a small serrated knife, cut the casing lengthwise, being careful not to cut through the sausage to protect your fingers.

2 Remove the casing from the meat. Compost the empty casing.

3 Crush the sausage meat in the skillet.

CHOOSE YOUR FAVE VEGGIES

Before cooking your sausage, brown vegetables (see Brown in Glossary p. 190) like mushrooms, onions and bell peppers to fill your sub.

Burger Tacos

WHEN THIS RECIPE STARTED TRENDING ON SOCIAL MEDIA, WE HAD TO TRY IT! AND TRUST US—THIS TASTY MEAL ISN'T JUST A PASSING FAD.

- -

preparation 25 minutes / **cooking** 10 minutes / **servings** 4

½ lb	(225 g) medium-lean ground beef
¼ cup	(40 g) finely chopped onion
½ tsp	garlic salt
4	soft wheat tortillas, each 7 inches (18 cm) in diameter
1 tbsp	(15 ml) vegetable oil
4	slices orange cheddar cheese
¼ cup	(60 ml) burger sauce, or more to taste (recipe opposite)
1 cup	(60 g) thinly sliced iceberg lettuce
¼ cup	(35 g) finely chopped dill pickle

1 In a bowl, combine the meat, onion and garlic salt. Season with salt and pepper.

2 Place about ¼ cup (60 ml) of the meat mixture on each tortilla. Lightly press on the meat so it covers most of the surface and sticks to the tortillas.

3 Lightly oil two non-stick skillets. Over medium heat, cook one taco at a time in each skillet, meat-side down for the first 2 minutes. Press on the tortillas with a spatula to release the meat juices.

4 Flip the tacos over and top each one with a slice of cheese. Continue to cook for 1 to 2 minutes or until the meat is cooked through and the cheese is melting.

5 Serve immediately with the burger sauce, lettuce and pickles. Fold the tacos in half to eat!

Burger Sauce

SWEET AND TANGY, THIS HOMEMADE ORANGE SAUCE IS WAY BETTER THAN THE ONE YOU GET IN YOUR FAST-FOOD BURGER!

- -

preparation 15 minutes / **makes about** 1 cup (250 ml)

¾ cup	(180 ml) mayonnaise
¼ cup	(40 g) finely chopped onion
1 tbsp	(15 ml) store-bought French dressing
1 tbsp	(15 ml) sweet relish
1 tbsp	finely chopped dill pickle
1 tsp	brown sugar
1 tsp	(5 ml) ketchup
1 tsp	(5 ml) white vinegar

1 In a bowl, combine all of the ingredients. Season with salt and pepper. The burger sauce will keep for 1 week in an airtight container in the refrigerator.

YUMMY MASHUPS

Just like mixing burgers and tacos together, you can make fun food combos like pizza bagels, sushi burritos or nacho fries. Which one's your favorite?

A TRICK THAT MEASURES UP

If you need to thaw frozen peas and corn, just put them in a bowl of cold water for 5 minutes, and then drain.

Chicken Fried Rice

LEFTOVERS DON'T HAVE TO BE BORING! GRAB LAST NIGHT'S CHICKEN AND RICE AND TURN THEM INTO SOMETHING NEW. RAID YOUR FRIDGE FOR MORE INGREDIENTS AND LET YOUR CREATIVITY RUN FREE!

preparation 20 minutes / **cooking** 13 minutes / **servings** 2

SAUCE

2 tbsp	(30 ml) low-sodium soy sauce
2 tbsp	(30 ml) mirin
2 tsp	(10 ml) toasted sesame oil

FRIED RICE

1	carrot, grated
4	green onions, thinly sliced, white and green parts separated
2 tbsp	(30 ml) vegetable oil
2	garlic cloves, finely chopped
2	eggs, lightly beaten
2 cups	(300 g) cooked long-grain parboiled rice (for cooking instructions, see the Burrito Bowls recipe p. 104, but use only ⅔ cup/135 g raw rice)
1 cup	(170 g) diced cooked chicken
½ cup	(75 g) frozen corn kernels, thawed (see A Trick That Measures Up p. 96)
½ cup	(75 g) frozen green peas, thawed (see A Trick That Measures Up p. 96)

SAUCE

1 In a small bowl, combine all of the ingredients. Set aside.

FRIED RICE

2 In a wok or large non-stick skillet over high heat, soften the carrot and white parts of the green onions in the oil. Add the garlic and continue to cook for 1 minute while stirring. Add the beaten eggs and continue to cook, breaking them up with a wooden spoon.

3 Add the rice and the sauce to the wok. Cook for 3 to 4 minutes or until the rice is slightly golden, stirring often.

4 Add the chicken, corn and peas to the wok. Cook for 2 to 3 minutes, stirring, to reheat the chicken and vegetables.

5 Divide the fried rice between two bowls. Garnish with the green parts of the green onions, to taste.

MEET MIRIN

Mirin is a sweet and tangy cooking sauce from Japan that's made from rice. It's like a syrupy vinegar, but instead of being sour, it's sweet. You'll often see it used in marinades, sauces and fried rice.

THE ART OF IMPROV

Throwing a meal together using leftovers is a fun way to get creative and reduce food waste. Try these ideas:

> **Put leftover meat in a sandwich.**

> **Use ripe bananas to bake Banana Muffins (p. 61).**

> **Turn old bread into croutons for a Caesar Salad (p. 80).**

A+ LUNCHES

CHICKEN AND
CRANBERRY WRAPS

CURRIED TUNA
SALAD WRAPS

PASTA SALAD
WITH TUNA

Pasta Salad with Tuna

CANNED TUNA IS SUPER HANDY! YOU CAN MIX IT INTO PASTA OR SALADS, OR EVEN MAKE IT INTO YUMMY TUNA PATTIES. EVERYONE HAS THEIR OWN FAVE WAY TO EAT IT.

preparation 20 minutes / cooking 10 minutes / servings 4

¾ lb	(340 g) fusilli or penne
2 cups	(300 g) frozen corn kernels
3 tbsp	(45 ml) vegetable oil
1 tsp	(5 ml) honey
1	lime, juiced
2 cups	(280 g) cherry tomatoes, halved
4 oz	(115 g) mini bocconcini
3	green onions, thinly sliced
1 can	(7 oz/198 g) oil-packed tuna, drained
½	English cucumber, quartered lengthwise, then thinly sliced crosswise
2 tbsp	finely chopped basil or flat-leaf parsley leaves

1 In a large pot of salted boiling water, cook the pasta until very al dente (see Very Al Dente). Add the corn and continue to cook for 2 minutes. Drain the pasta and corn. Let cool.

2 In a salad bowl or large bowl, whisk together the oil, honey and lime juice. Season with salt and pepper. Add the remaining ingredients, pasta and corn. Mix well.

3 Serve immediately, or cover and refrigerate until ready to serve.

VERY AL DENTE
If you like your pasta a little chewy (very al dente!), cook it 2 minutes less than package instructions (see Al Dente p. 69).

Chicken and Cranberry Wraps

ENJOY THIS TASTY CHICKEN FILLING IN A WRAP OR EAT IT WITH CRACKERS AS A YUMMY SALAD SNACK.

preparation 25 minutes / servings 4

CHICKEN FILLING

1½ cups	(255 g) coarsely chopped cooked chicken
½ cup	(75 g) dried cranberries
2	celery stalks, diced
⅓ cup	(75 ml) mayonnaise or sour cream
2 tbsp	(30 ml) whole-grain mustard
2 tbsp	finely chopped dill

WRAPS

4	soft wheat tortillas, each 10 inches (25 cm) in diameter
	Mayonnaise or sour cream, to taste
2 cups	(50 g) baby spinach
1	Cortland apple, cored and julienned

CHICKEN FILLING

1 In a bowl, combine all of the ingredients. Season with salt and pepper.

WRAPS

2 Place the tortillas on a work surface. Spread with mayonnaise. On the bottom half of each tortilla, place the spinach, chicken filling and apple.

3 Fold the two opposite sides of each tortilla in toward the center, then firmly roll up from the bottom toward the top to hold in the filling (see The Foolproof Way to Fold a Wrap p. 101).

4 Individually cover each wrap with parchment paper, twisting each end of the paper to seal. Cut the wraps in half, if desired.

JULIENNE
This is a fun way to chop fruits and veggies into tiny matchstick-sized pieces.

Curried Tuna Salad Wraps

IT'S TIME FOR LUNCH, AND GUESS WHAT? YOU MADE YOUR OWN TUNA SALAD WRAP! (YES, THAT'S A MAJOR FLEX.)

preparation 20 minutes / **servings** 4

TUNA FILLING

2 cans	(7 oz/198 g each) oil-packed tuna, drained
⅓ cup	(75 ml) mayonnaise
¼ cup	(40 g) finely chopped red onion
¼ cup	(35 g) small-diced celery
1 tbsp	small-diced sweet pickle
½ tsp	curry powder

WRAPS

4	soft wheat tortillas, each 10 inches (25 cm) in diameter
4 tsp	(20 ml) honey
	Boston lettuce leaves, to taste

TUNA FILLING

1 In a bowl, combine all of the ingredients. Season with pepper.

WRAPS

2 Place the tortillas on a work surface. Cover the bottom half of each tortilla with honey (see The Magic of Honey). Top with lettuce leaves and the tuna filling.

3 Fold the two opposite sides of each tortilla in toward the center, then firmly roll up from the bottom toward the top to hold in the filling (see The Foolproof Way to Fold a Wrap).

4 Individually cover each wrap with parchment paper, twisting each end of the paper to seal. Cut the wraps in half, if desired.

THE MAGIC OF HONEY

Ever tried honey in a wrap? Not only is it sweet, but it also helps keep the filling in place by sticking to the tortilla.

THE FOOLPROOF
WAY TO FOLD A WRAP

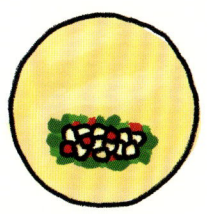

> Put all your ingredients at the bottom of the tortilla.

> Fold the left and right sides over.

> Fold the bottom part up over the filling.

> Start rolling up the tortilla while pressing down firmly. Be sure to roll it up tight!

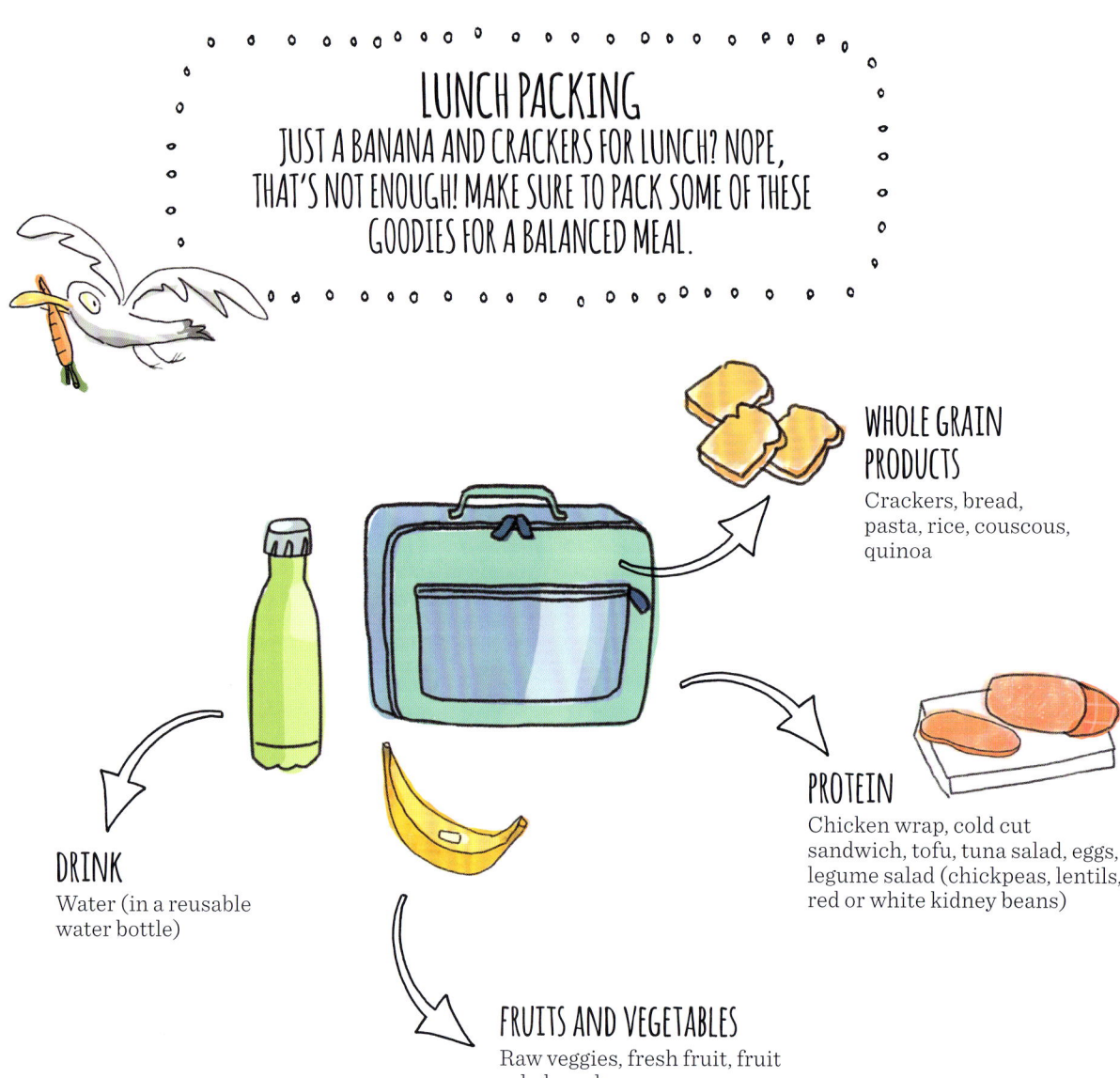

LUNCH PACKING
JUST A BANANA AND CRACKERS FOR LUNCH? NOPE, THAT'S NOT ENOUGH! MAKE SURE TO PACK SOME OF THESE GOODIES FOR A BALANCED MEAL.

WHOLE GRAIN PRODUCTS
Crackers, bread, pasta, rice, couscous, quinoa

PROTEIN
Chicken wrap, cold cut sandwich, tofu, tuna salad, eggs, legume salad (chickpeas, lentils, red or white kidney beans)

DRINK
Water (in a reusable water bottle)

FRUITS AND VEGETABLES
Raw veggies, fresh fruit, fruit salad, applesauce

LUNCHTIME HERO

GOT A MICROWAVE AT SCHOOL?

YES   **NO**

DO YOU HAVE COLD CUTS OR LEFTOVER COOKED MEAT IN THE FRIDGE?

NO   **YES**

Put last night's dinner leftovers in your lunch box.

DO YOU HAVE ANY CANNED GOODS IN THE PANTRY?

YES   **NO**

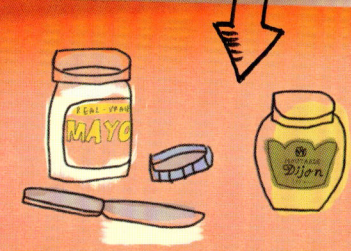

PERFECT!

Make a sandwich using your favorite condiments (pesto, mayo, mustard, hummus, hot sauce and so on).

YUM!

You can make:
- a wrap, like Chicken and Cranberry (p. 100) or Curried Tuna Salad (p. 101)
- Pasta Salad with Tuna (p. 100)
- a salad with legumes and canned veggies

IT'S PROBABLY TIME TO GO TO THE GROCERY STORE.

Burrito Bowls

IT'S A FIESTA IN A BOWL! IF YOU'RE TIRED OF BROKEN TACO SHELLS, PUT ALL YOUR TACO FILLINGS IN A BOWL FOR A MESS-FREE LUNCH.

- -

preparation 35 minutes / **cooking** 25 minutes / **servings** 4

RICE

2 cups	(500 ml) water
½ tsp	salt
1 cup	(200 g) long-grain parboiled rice

MEAT

¾ lb	(340 g) lean ground beef
2 tbsp	(30 ml) vegetable oil
2 tsp	chili powder
1 tsp	onion salt
3 tbsp	(45 ml) chili sauce

CORN SALAD

1	tomato, diced
1 can	1¼ cups (215 g) canned corn kernels, drained
½ cup	(90 g) canned black beans, rinsed and drained
¼ cup	(10 g) finely chopped cilantro leaves

BOWLS

1 cup	(100 g) grated sharp orange cheddar cheese
1	large avocado, ripe but firm, halved and pitted (see Cheesy Avocado Dip p. 47, steps 1 to 2)
	Sour cream, to taste
	Lime wedges, to taste

RICE

1 In a pot, bring the water and salt to a boil. Add the rice and stir with a wooden spoon. Reduce the heat to low. Cover and cook for 18 minutes. Remove from the heat and let sit, covered, for 5 minutes. Remove the lid and fluff the grains of rice with a fork (see Rice Made Easy).

MEAT

2 Before starting, read "How to cook ground meat!" on page 109. In a large non-stick skillet over medium-high heat, cook the meat in the oil with the spices, breaking the meat up with a wooden spoon, for 8 minutes or until nicely browned. Add the chili sauce and continue to cook for 30 seconds while stirring. Keep warm.

CORN SALAD

3 In a bowl, combine all of the ingredients. Season with salt and pepper.

BOWLS

4 Divide the rice, meat mixture and corn salad among four bowls. Top with the cheese, pieces of avocado removed with a spoon and sour cream. Drizzle with lime juice.

RICE MADE EASY

Use a rice cooker to make the perfect rice—just follow the instructions in the booklet!

PSST!

Want to get more juice out of a lime? Roll it on the counter while pressing down with your palm first, then cut it in half and squeeze away!

A ONE-POT MEAL A DAY KEEPS PILES OF DIRTY DISHES AWAY!

Pork Casserole for Tortillas

A TASTY FAJITA FILLING THAT YOU CAN SERVE DIRECTLY OUT OF THE SKILLET? EASY PEASY!

preparation 25 minutes / **cooking** 30 minutes / **servings** 8

1 lb	(450 g) lean ground pork	
1	onion, chopped	
2	garlic cloves, finely chopped	
1 tbsp	(15 ml) vegetable oil	
2	bell peppers, various colors, seeded and diced	
4 cups	(400 g) small cauliflower florets	
1 can	(28 oz/796 ml) diced plum tomatoes	
1 can	(19 oz/540 ml) small black or red beans, rinsed and drained	
1 tbsp	chili powder	
1 tsp	ground coriander seeds	
2 cups	(200 g) grated marbled cheddar cheese (mild or sharp)	
3 tbsp	finely chopped cilantro	
8	soft wheat tortillas, each about 7 inches (18 cm) in diameter	
	Sour cream, to taste	

1 Before starting, read "How to Cook Ground Meat!" on page 109. In a large non-stick skillet over medium-high heat, cook the meat, onion and garlic in the oil, breaking the meat up with a wooden spoon, for 8 minutes or until nicely browned. Season with salt and pepper.

2 Add the bell peppers and cauliflower to the skillet. Continue to cook for 5 minutes while stirring often.

3 Add the tomatoes, beans and spices to the skillet. Mix well. Simmer for 10 minutes or until the vegetables are tender and the sauce has thickened.

4 Sprinkle with the cheese. Cover and continue to cook over low heat until the cheese has completely melted, about 3 minutes.

5 Remove from the oven and garnish with the cilantro. Serve with the tortillas and sour cream.

Tex-Mex

UNITED STATES

TEXAS

MEXICO

TEXAN INSPO

Surprise: it turns out that nachos aren't really a Mexican dish! They actually come from Tex-Mex food, which is found in Texas. Texas borders Mexico, so Tex-Mex food is pretty much Mexican food with an American twist. Tex-Mex usually uses shredded cheese and flour tortillas instead of corn ones!

TEX-MEX FAV

- Nachos
- Chili con carne
- Fajitas
- Quesadillas
- Cheese sauce (queso)

Cheeseburger Nachos

WHAT HAPPENS WHEN YOU CAN'T PICK BETWEEN YOUR TWO FAVOURITE DISHES? YOU MIX THEM TOGETHER FOR THE ULTIMATE COMBO, OF COURSE!

- -

preparation 20 minutes / **cooking** 20 minutes / **servings** 4

1 lb	(450 g) medium-lean ground beef
2 tbsp	(30 ml) vegetable oil
3 tbsp	(45 ml) ketchup
10 cups	(250 g) yellow corn chips
2 cups	(200 g) grated sharp orange cheddar cheese
1½ cups	(90 g) thinly sliced iceberg lettuce
1	tomato, diced
	Round slices dill pickle, to taste
1	recipe Cheese Sauce, hot (recipe opposite)

1 With the rack in the middle position, preheat the oven to 425°F (220°C). Line a baking sheet with parchment paper.

2 Before starting, read "How to Cook Ground Meat!" In a large non-stick skillet over medium-high heat, cook the meat in the oil, breaking it up with a wooden spoon, for 8 minutes or until nicely browned. Season with salt and pepper. Add the ketchup and continue to cook for 2 minutes while stirring. Remove from the heat.

3 Spread the corn chips out on the baking sheet. Top with the grated cheese and the meat mixture. Bake for 8 minutes or until the cheese has completely melted.

4 Remove the baking sheet from the oven. Garnish the nachos with the lettuce, diced tomato and pickle slices. Drizzle with some of the cheese sauce.

5 Place the baking sheet in the center of the table. Serve with the remaining cheese sauce. Serve immediately.

HOW TO COOK GROUND MEAT!

1 In a large non-stick skillet over medium-high heat, warm the oil. Spread the ground meat out in the skillet without overcrowding it.

2 Using a wooden spoon, break the meat up without stirring. Once the meat is golden on one side, flip it over while continuing to break it up.

3 Once the meat is nicely browned on all sides, continue with the recipe.

Cheese Sauce

CHIPS AND SAUCE ARE THE PERFECT PAIR. WITH THIS RECIPE, YOU'LL ALWAYS HAVE ENOUGH SAUCE TO DRIZZLE OVER YOUR NACHOS.

- -

preparation 10 minutes / **cooking** 5 minutes
makes about 1 cup (250 ml)

½ cup	(125 ml) milk
1 tsp	cornstarch
¼ tsp	salt
¼ tsp	onion powder
¼ tsp	sweet paprika
1½ cups	(150 g) grated sharp orange cheddar cheese

1 In a pot off the heat, whisk together the milk, cornstarch, salt and spices. Bring to a boil over medium heat, stirring constantly and scraping the bottom and sides of the pot. Simmer for 1 minute. Remove from the heat.

2 Add the cheese to the pot and whisk to combine. Reheat over low heat, as needed, being careful not to boil the sauce.

3 The cheese sauce will keep for 1 week in an airtight container in the refrigerator.

TOO MUCH SAUCE? NEVER!

Breaded fish sticks

EAt THEM WITH
YOUR FINGERS!

Crispy tofu sticks

Breaded Fish Sticks

TELL THE FAM THIS RECIPE WAS INSPIRED BY BRITISH FISH AND CHIPS, AND THEY'LL THINK YOU'RE SUCH A COOKING PRO!

- -

preparation 20 minutes / **cooking** 10 minutes / **servings** 4

½ cup	(75 g) unbleached all-purpose flour
3	eggs
2 cups	(160 g) panko breadcrumbs
½ tsp	onion powder (optional)
1½ lb	(675 g) haddock fillets, patted dry and cut into sticks about 1 inch (2.5 cm) wide x 4 inches (10 cm) long
¾ cup	(180 ml) vegetable oil

1 Place the flour in a shallow dish. In a second shallow dish, lightly beat the eggs. In a third shallow dish, combine the breadcrumbs and onion powder.

2 Season the fish sticks with salt and pepper. Dredge the fish in the flour, shaking off any excess. Dip into the beaten eggs, letting some of the excess drip off. Press into the breadcrumb mixture to coat well.

3 In a non-stick skillet over medium heat, warm the oil for 2 minutes (see Careful!). Cook half of the fish sticks at a time in the hot oil for 2 to 3 minutes on each side or until golden all over. Watch out for splattering oil. Drain on a plate lined with paper towels. Add more oil to the skillet as needed.

4 Divide the fish sticks among four plates. Serve with Tartare Sauce (recipe opposite).

Tartare Sauce

NO, SILLY: TARTARE SAUCE DOESN'T INCLUDE TARTAR FROM YOUR TEETH! WE PROMISE. BUT AS ALWAYS, BE SURE TO BRUSH YOUR TEETH AFTER YOU EAT!

- -

preparation 5 minutes / **makes** ¾ cup (180 ml)

½ cup	(125 ml) mayonnaise
1 tbsp	(15 ml) lemon juice
1 tbsp	(15 ml) whole-grain mustard
1 tbsp	(15 ml) sweet relish
1 tbsp	finely chopped sweet pickle

1 In a small bowl, combine all of the ingredients. Season with salt and pepper. The tartare sauce will keep for 1 week in an airtight container in the refrigerator.

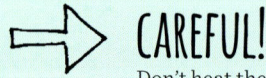 CAREFUL!

Don't heat the oil for too long, or it could burn the coating before the fish is cooked.

PANKO

These are a kind of Japanese breadcrumbs that are light and flaky. You can find them in most grocery stores!

Crispy Tofu Sticks

DON'T LIKE FISH? HERE'S A SOLUTION: REPLACE IT WITH TOFU! THESE ARE JUST AS TASTY AS FISH STICKS.

preparation 35 minutes / **cooking** 18 minutes / **servings** 4

SAUCE

½ cup	(125 ml) mayonnaise
2 tbsp	(30 ml) low-sodium soy sauce
1 tbsp	(15 ml) maple syrup
1 tbsp	(15 ml) toasted sesame oil
1 tsp	(5 ml) sambal oelek

TOFU

¼ cup	(35 g) cornstarch
1½ cups	(120 g) panko breadcrumbs
1 tbsp	(15 ml) vegetable oil
1 lb	(450 g) firm tofu, patted dry and cut into 3 × ¾ × ½-inch (7.5 × 2 × 1 cm) sticks

SAUCE

1 In a shallow dish, whisk together all of the ingredients. Season lightly with pepper. Transfer ½ cup (125 ml) of the sauce to a small bowl. Cover and refrigerate until ready to serve. Set aside the shallow dish of remaining sauce.

TOFU

2 With the rack in the middle position, preheat the oven to 425°F (220°C).

3 Place the cornstarch in another shallow dish. In a third shallow dish, combine the breadcrumbs and oil.

4 Dredge the tofu sticks in the cornstarch, shaking off any excess. Dip into the reserved sauce, letting some of the excess drip off. Press into the breadcrumb mixture to coat well. Place the coated tofu sticks on a non-stick or parchment paper–lined baking sheet.

5 Bake for 18 to 20 minutes or until the tofu sticks are golden.

6 Divide the tofu sticks among four plates. Serve with the reserved mayonnaise sauce. Delicious served with green beans.

TOFU THROUGH AND THROUGH

Tofu is a solid white block that you may find in the grocery store near the produce section. You can use it as a meat replacement in a bunch of dishes you already love, like fish sticks, stir-fries or even burger patties! It doesn't have a lot of flavor, so be sure to coat, season or marinate it until it's super tasty!

BUT WHAT EXACTLY IS IT?

Scientifically, tofu is a plant-based protein made of soy milk that's been thickened up and then turned into a block. Proteins are what give you the energy to walk, dance and watch a few too many reels on TikTok.

WHAT'S an AIR FRYER?

You've probably heard of air fryers before, and may already have one sitting on your kitchen counter! It's like a tiny oven with a super strong fan that pushes hot air around to cook foods quickly. It's especially great at making foods crispy without having to dunk them in oil. Your air fryer may include functions like "Cook," "Roast" and "Dehydrate," and you can also cook veggies, meats and even desserts in it!

Air Fryer General Tso's Tofu

BIG FAN OF TAKEOUT GENERAL TSO'S CHICKEN? WE HOPE IT DOESN'T TAKE TOO MUCH CONVINCING FOR YOU TO TRY THIS TOFU VERSION! IT'S VERY YUMMY AND COOKS SUPER FAST THANKS TO THE AIR FRYER.

preparation 20 minutes / **cooking** 16 minutes / **servings** 4

TOFU

1 lb	(450 g) firm tofu, cubed
1 tbsp	(15 ml) vegetable oil
3 tbsp	cornstarch

SAUCE

3 tbsp	(45 ml) maple syrup
2 tbsp	(30 ml) ketchup
2 tbsp	(30 ml) hoisin sauce
1 tbsp	(15 ml) low-sodium soy sauce
1 tbsp	(15 ml) toasted sesame oil
1 tbsp	chopped fresh ginger
1 tsp	(5 ml) sambal oelek
2	garlic cloves, finely chopped
2	green onions, cut into pieces ¾ inch (2 cm) long

TOFU

1 In a large bowl, toss the tofu with the oil. Add the cornstarch and mix to coat the tofu well. Season with salt and pepper.

2 Spread the tofu out in the basket of an air fryer. Cook for 10 minutes at 400°F (200°C). Stir the tofu and continue to cook for 5 minutes or until slightly crispy (see Adapt Your Cooking Time).

SAUCE

3 Meanwhile, in a non-stick skillet, bring all of the ingredients except for the green onions to a boil. Simmer for 1 minute.

4 Add the tofu and green onions to the skillet. Simmer for 1 minute, stirring, until the tofu is nicely glazed with the sauce.

5 Divide the tofu among four plates. Serve with white rice and a green vegetable, if desired.

ADAPT
YOUR COOKING TIME
The air fryer's strength varies from one manufacturer to the next, so cooking times can be different.

GIVE YOUR OVEN A VACATION

BLANCH

This means cooking veggies in boiling water for 1 or 2 minutes so they can soften, and then dunking them in ice water to stop the cooking process. Blanching helps veggies keep their crunch and color.

SEASONED MAYONNAISE

In a small bowl, mix with a whisk ½ cup (125 ml) mayonnaise, 2 tbsp (30 ml) mirin (or 1 tbsp /15 ml maple syrup) and 2 tsp (10 ml) sriracha.

Salmon Poke Bowls

POKE BOWLS COME FROM HAWAII AND THIS VERSION LETS YOU ADD ALMOST ANY INGREDIENT YOU WANT! YOU'LL BE SWIMMING IN AN OCEAN OF POSSIBILITY...

preparation 30 minutes / **cooking** 2 minutes
chilling 15 minutes / **servings** 4

SALMON
¾ lb	(340 g) salmon fillet without skin
1 tbsp	(15 ml) vegetable oil
1 tbsp	(15 ml) toasted sesame oil

BOWLS
1	recipe cooked Sushi Rice (recipe opposite)
1½ cups	(220 g) frozen shelled edamame, blanched for 3 minutes
2	carrots, grated
2	Lebanese cucumbers, halved lengthwise, then thinly sliced into halfmoons
1	avocado, ripe but firm, diced (see Cheesy Avocado Dip recipe p. 47, steps 1 and 2)
1	mango, ripe but firm, peeled and diced
1	romaine lettuce heart, thinly sliced
2	green onions, thinly sliced
	Roasted sesame seeds, to taste

SALMON

1 Place the salmon in a glass or ceramic baking dish. Coat with both the vegetable and sesame oils. Season with salt and pepper.

2 Cover the baking dish with plastic wrap. Cook in the microwave oven for 2 minutes, 1 minute at a time, until just cooked (see All About Poke).

3 Remove the plastic wrap. Using a large spatula, remove the salmon from the baking dish and transfer to a plate. Refrigerate for 15 minutes or until slightly cooled. Drain the salmon as needed. Break up into pieces.

BOWLS

4 Divide the rice among four bowls. Top with the salmon, edamame, carrots, cucumbers, avocado, mango, lettuce and green onions. Sprinkle with sesame seeds. Serve with seasoned mayonnaise.

Sushi Rice

TO MAKE THE BEST POKE BOWLS YOU'LL DEFINITELY NEED SOME STICKY RICE THAT YOU CAN PICK UP WITH CHOPSTICKS.

preparation 15 minutes / **cooking** 25 minutes / **servings** 4

1½ cups	(325 g) Calrose rice (sushi rice)
1¾ cups	(430 ml) water
½ tsp	salt

1 Rinse the rice under cold running water until the water runs clear. Drain well.

2 In a pot, bring the rice, water and salt to a boil. Reduce the heat to low. Cover and cook for 15 minutes or until the water has been completely absorbed by the rice. Remove from the heat and let rest for 10 minutes, covered (see There's Another Way).

3 Remove the lid and fluff the grains of rice with a fork. Let cool.

THERE'S ANOTHER WAY

You can also use a rice cooker to make rice—just follow the instructions in the booklet!

ALL ABOUT POKE

> This recipe uses cooked fish, but if you want to try a traditional poke using raw fish, be sure to ask your grown-up or local fishmonger to make sure it's super fresh!

> Once cooked, the fish will have a white coating on the outside—this is a protein that's pushed to the surface of the salmon when heated—and pink on the inside.

MAKE YOUR OWN POKE

SALMON

TUNA

NORTHERN SHRIMP

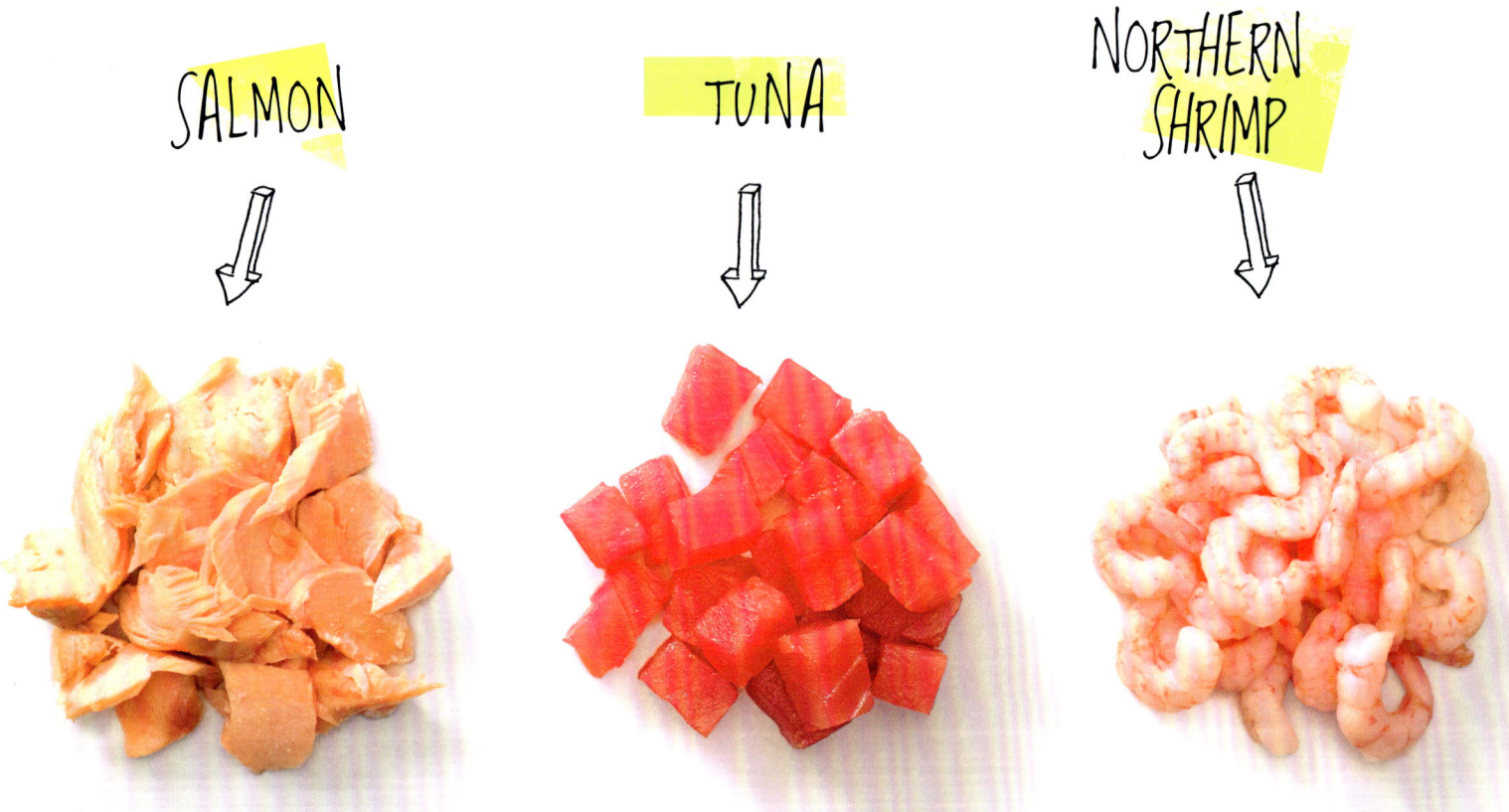

Aloha! Once you've got your sushi rice ready, let your imagination run wild to create a poke bowl just the way you want it. Use your fave fish or seafood, and mix in different veggies like sliced radishes, bell pepper sticks or chopped cabbage. Don't be afraid to add fruits too, like some pineapple or diced mango on top!

pineapple

edamame

avocado

sesame seeds

spring mix

bell pepper

red onion

green or red cabbage

mango

radishes

cucumber

sushi rice

green onion

carrots

lettuce

119

Cheesy Ramen Noodles

GET READY FOR A HISTORIC MEETING BETWEEN RAMEN AND MAC AND CHEESE! IN JUST A FEW MINUTES, YOU'RE IN FOR AN EXPLOSION OF FLAVOR!

preparation 10 minutes / **cooking** 8 minutes / **servings** 2

2	packages (3 oz/85 g each) instant ramen noodles, without the packet of seasoning (see Packet Free)
2 tbsp	butter
½ tsp	dry mustard
½ tsp	chili powder
¼ tsp	onion powder
½ cup	(125 ml) milk
½ cup	(50 g) grated sharp orange cheddar cheese (see As Long as There's Cheese)
2 tbsp	finely chopped chives

1 In a pot of salted boiling water, cook the ramen until al dente, about 2 to 3 minutes, stirring to separate the noodles. Drain the noodles and lightly oil.

2 In the same pot over medium heat, melt the butter. Add the spices and cook for 1 minute while stirring with a whisk. Pour in the milk. Bring to a boil while whisking constantly.

3 Add the cheese and noodles to the pot. Cook for 2 minutes or until the cheese has melted, stirring constantly. Season with salt and pepper.

4 Divide the noodles between two bowls. Sprinkle with the chives. Serve immediately.

PACKET FREE

You don't need to use the seasoning packets that come with instant noodles for this recipe. But if you want to use them, just leave out the dry mustard, chili powder, onion powder and salt and pepper included in the ingredients list.

AS LONG AS THERE'S CHEESE

This recipe will also taste great with mozzarella!

HARD-BOILED EGGS

Place the eggs in a small pot and cover with warm water. Bring to a boil. Cover and remove from the heat. Let sit for 10 minutes. Drain the eggs and fill the pot with cold water. Return the eggs to the pot and let cool for 5 minutes. Peel the eggs under cold running water and pat dry. Compost the shells.

Ramen Soup with Tofu

THIS COMFORTING AND NOURISHING SOUP IS SURE TO BRING A SMILE TO EVERYONE AT THE TABLE. AND REMEMBER: IT'S OK TO SLURP!

preparation 20 minutes / **cooking** 15 minutes / **servings** 4

3	packages (3 oz/85 g each) instant ramen noodles, without the packet of seasoning (see Packet Free p. 120)
6 cups	(1.5 L) chicken broth
3 tbsp	(45 ml) low-sodium soy sauce
1	red bell pepper, seeded and thinly sliced
¼ lb	(115 g) snow peas, trimmed
¼ lb	(115 g) white or shiitake mushrooms, stems removed, caps thinly sliced
¾ lb	(340 g) cubed medium-firm tofu, patted dry
2	green onions, thinly sliced
4	hard-boiled eggs, halved (see Hard-Boiled Eggs p. 122)

1 In a pot of salted boiling water, cook the ramen until al dente, about 2 to 3 minutes, stirring to separate the noodles. Drain the noodles and lightly oil. Set aside.

2 In the same pot, bring the broth and soy sauce to a boil. Add the bell pepper, snow peas and mushrooms. Simmer for 1 minute. Add the tofu and green onions. Remove from the heat.

3 Divide the noodles among four bowls. Top with the vegetables, tofu and broth. Add two egg halves to each bowl. Serve immediately.

EVEN MORE TASTY
You can also add leftover cooked chicken to your soup!

TRIM

This means to remove the parts you don't want to eat from a food before cooking (like the dry ends of snow peas!).

Quick Butter Chicken

SKIP DELIVERY TONIGHT. WHY? BECAUSE YOU CAN MAKE A QUICK INDIAN-INSPIRED BUTTER CHICKEN IN JUST THREE EASY STEPS!

preparation 15 minutes / **cooking** 20 minutes / **servings** 4

1½ lb	(675 g) boneless, skinless chicken thighs, cut into pieces (see Tofu Version)
3 tbsp	butter
1 tbsp	curry powder
½ tsp	garlic powder
1 can	(10 oz/284 ml) condensed tomato soup, undiluted
10 oz	(284 ml) milk (measured in the soup can)
	Cilantro leaves, for serving

1 In a large non-stick skillet over high heat, brown half of the chicken at a time in half of the butter (1½ tbsp) with the curry powder and garlic powder. Set aside on a plate.

2 Add the tomato soup and milk to the skillet. Mix well. Return the chicken to the skillet. Bring to a boil while stirring. Simmer gently for 8 to 10 minutes or until the sauce is very thick. Season with pepper.

3 Divide the butter chicken among four plates. Garnish with cilantro leaves. Serve with white rice and naan bread, if desired.

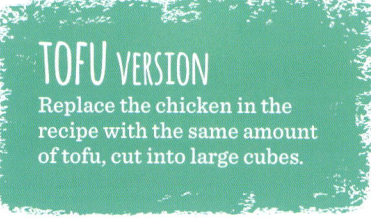

TOFU VERSION
Replace the chicken in the recipe with the same amount of tofu, cut into large cubes.

CHAPTER 04

I'M THIRSTY!

GET READY TO SIP ON SOMETHING TRULY FUN! WE'VE GOT DRINKS FOR EVERY OCCASION THAT ARE WAY MORE EXCITING THAN YOUR USUAL FRUIT JUICE. WHETHER YOU'RE BY THE POOL OR AT THE SKATING RINK, YOU'LL ALWAYS HAVE SOMETHING YUMMY TO DRINK.

SPARKLE & FIZZ

If you have a machine for making sparkling water at home, set it to the highest setting (AKA the most bubbles). Once you add the orange syrup, some bubbles may disappear, so make sure to go big!

COLOR EXPLOSION

Want your drink to look and taste like orange soda from the store? Just add a bit of grenadine syrup for a fruity taste and bright color.

Homemade Orange Soda

THIS FIZZY ORANGE SODA IS MADE WITH REAL ORANGE JUICE AND TASTES WAY BETTER THAN THE STORE-BOUGHT STUFF. PLUS, IT'S HEALTHIER!

preparation 25 minutes / **cooking** 10 minutes
chilling 1 hour / **servings** 7 to 8

ORANGE SYRUP

1 cup	(210 g) sugar
2	oranges, zest only, finely grated (see Glossary p. 193)
1½ cups	(375 ml) orange juice (about 4 oranges)
2 tbsp	(30 ml) lemon juice

SODA

¼ cup	(60 ml) grenadine syrup (optional)
	Ice cubes
4 cups	(1 L) cold sparkling water or club soda
7 or 8	halfmoon orange slices, for serving

ORANGE SYRUP

1 In a small pot, bring all of the ingredients to a boil. Simmer over low heat for 3 minutes. Transfer to a bowl and let cool. Cover and refrigerate for 1 hour or until the syrup has completely chilled.

2 Strain the syrup through a sieve placed over a large measuring cup or bowl, pressing on the zest with the back of a ladle to extract as much liquid as possible. Compost the orange zest. The syrup will keep for 1 month in an airtight container in the refrigerator.

SODA

3 In each glass, combine ¼ cup (60 ml) of the orange syrup and 1½ tsp (7.5 ml) of the grenadine. Fill each glass three-quarters of the way up with ice cubes. Top off with the sparkling water. Using a spoon, stir gently. Garnish each glass with an orange slice.

WITH GRENADINE SYRUP

{ YOUR AT-HOME ICE CREAM STORE }

MAKING SLUSHIES, MILKSHAKES AND OTHER COLD
DRINKS AT HOME IS PRETTY COOL! YOU WON'T EVEN
MISS THE TREATS FROM THE ICE CREAM STORE AS
YOURS WILL BE EVEN TASTIER!

Strawberry SLUSH

pineapple-coconut SMOOTHIE

To help the planet, use a reusable or biodegradable straw instead of a plastic one. Doing this means you're drinking in a "green" way, even if your drink isn't green in color!

strawberry–banana

blueberry–
blackberry

mango

Fruity
MILKSHAKES

Strawberry Slush

NOT LOVING THE BRIGHT NEON SLUSHIES FROM THE CONVENIENCE STORE ANYMORE? TRY CRUSHING FROZEN STRAWBERRIES INSTEAD FOR A COOL PINK DRINK, NO FOOD DYE REQUIRED!

preparation 10 minutes / **servings** 4

3 cups	(420 g) frozen sliced strawberries
2 cups	(500 ml) water
¼ cup	(55 g) sugar
4	fresh strawberries, to decorate
4	thin lime wedges, to decorate

1 In a blender, purée the frozen strawberries, water and sugar until smooth.

2 Divide the slush among four glasses. Decorate with the fresh strawberries and lime wedges. Serve immediately with wide straws or spoons.

Pineapple-Coconut Smoothie

SMOOTHIES ARE CALLED "SMOOTHIES" BECAUSE THEY'RE SO SMOOTH AND EASY TO DRINK. AREN'T YOU GLAD THEY AREN'T CALLED "LUMPIES"?!

preparation 10 minutes / **servings** 2

1 cup	(145 g) frozen pineapple chunks
½ cup	(125 ml) pineapple or orange juice
½ cup	(125 ml) coconut milk
1 tbsp	(15 ml) lime juice
½	ripe banana, sliced

1 In a blender, purée all of the ingredients until smooth.

2 Divide the smoothie between two glasses. Serve immediately.

Q&A TIME WITH QUENTIN

HOW IS COCONUT MILK MADE?

The coconut milk you find at the store is made by squeezing grated coconuts and sometimes adding water. Coconut milk can separate into solid and liquid parts, so be sure to shake before using! You can also use the parts separately in soups, smoothies and sauces—just follow the recipe carefully.

Fruity Milkshake

YES, A MILKSHAKE IS STILL CALLED A "MILKSHAKE" WHEN YOU USE A BLENDER. IT'S A GOOD THING, TOO, BECAUSE SHAKING BY HAND WOULD MAKE YOUR ARMS GET SUPER TIRED!

preparation 15 minutes / **servings** 2

1 cup	(250 ml) milk
½ cup	(125 ml) store-bought or homemade Vanilla Ice Cream (recipe p. 146)
½ cup	(70 g) frozen sliced strawberries (see Choose Your Own Fruit)
1	small ripe banana, sliced
⅓ cup	(75 ml) 35% whipping cream (optional)

1 In a blender, purée the milk, ice cream and fruit until smooth. Divide the milkshake between two glasses.

2 In a bowl, whisk the 35% cream with an electric mixer on medium speed until stiff peaks form.

3 Top off the milkshakes with the whipped cream. Serve immediately with wide straws.

CHOOSE YOUR OWN FRUIT

Do you like strawberries, but *love* blueberries? No problem: this recipe can be made with all kinds of frozen fruit! Blueberries, raspberries, blackberries, mango...you'll want to try them all! (But maybe not all at the same time.)

CRUSH IT GOOD!

Don't you hate it when frozen fruit get stuck in the blade of the blender? Make sure to use the "Crush" button to break down and pulverize it! And, as always, don't forget the lid.

READY FOR A
BRAIN FREEZE?

Watermelon Lemonade Slush

FROZEN WATERMELON CUBES MAKE THE BEST SLUSHIES! EVEN WHEN THEY MELT, YOUR SLUSHIE WON'T BE WATERY.

preparation 20 minutes / **cooking** 5 minutes
freezing 4 hours / **servings** 4

4 cups	(600 g) cubed seedless watermelon (see both Chopping Your Watermelon and Mix Your Melons)
½ cup	(125 ml) water
½ cup	(125 ml) lemon juice
⅓ cup	(70 g) sugar

1 Line a baking sheet with a silicone mat or parchment paper. Place the melon cubes on the baking sheet and freeze for 4 hours or until frozen solid.

2 Meanwhile, in a small pot, bring the water, lemon juice and sugar to a boil. Simmer just until the sugar has dissolved. Transfer to a bowl and let cool. Cover and refrigerate until ready to use.

3 In a blender or food processor, purée the melon cubes with the cooled lemon syrup until thick and slushy.

4 Divide the slush among four glasses. Serve immediately with wide straws or spoons.

MIX YOUR MELONS

In this recipe, you can swap watermelon for honeydew or cantaloupe. Just make sure to use a super juicy fruit for that ultimate slushie feel!

CHOPPING YOUR WATERMELON

Careful! Watermelons can roll around on the cutting board. Make sure to ask a grown-up to help cut it in half for you. Put the flat side down on the board. To take off the rind, start at the top and cut down, only removing the green and white parts. Then chop the pink part into cubes! Repeat with the other half.

FREEZING TIP

When freezing your melon cubes, spread them out evenly on a baking sheet so they don't overlap. This keeps them from sticking together, making them easier to handle later!

TEA

MILK

PEARLS

STRAWBERRY SYRUP

Strawberry-Melon Bubble Tea

NO NEED TO GO TO THE MALL FOR BUBBLE TEA! GET YOUR FIX WITH THIS RECIPE AND YOUR FRIENDS WILL BE LINING UP OUTSIDE YOUR HOUSE.

preparation 10 minutes / **serving** 1

¼ cup	(35 g) fresh or frozen sliced strawberries (thawed if frozen)
¼ cup	(60 g) tapioca pearls, cooked and chilled (see In My Bubble)
2 tbsp	(30 ml) strawberry syrup, or more to taste (recipe opposite)
½ cup	(125 ml) homemade or store-bought unsweetened green tea, cold (see Don't Like Green Tea?)
½ cup	(125 ml) milk
¼ cup	(45 g) honeydew melon, peeled, seeded and cut into small dice

1 In a large glass, using a cocktail muddler, crush the strawberries to extract the juice. If you don't have a muddler, crush the strawberries in a small bowl with a fork. Transfer to a large glass and continue with the recipe.

2 Add the tapioca to the glass. Pour in the strawberry syrup, tea and milk. Garnish with the diced melon. Serve immediately with a wide straw.

DON'T LIKE GREEN TEA?
You can replace it with caffeine-free black tea or your favorite herbal tea.

IN MY BUBBLE
You can find tapioca pearls (also called boba pearls) in some grocery stores. They come in plain and fruity flavors. Some need to be cooked for a while, while others cook faster or just need water. Follow the directions on the package.

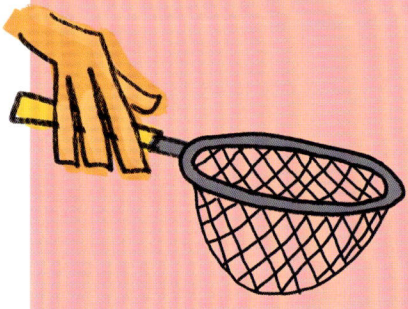

FEEL THE STRAIN

If you're using raspberries or strawberries, place a fine mesh strainer over a large measuring cup or bowl, and strain the yogurt mixture before serving. Don't forget to compost the seeds!

Some fruits are sweeter than others, so you can add more or less sugar based on how sweet you like it.

Yogurt and Fruit Drink

YOU DON'T HAVE TO ASK YOUR PARENTS TO BUY THESE DRINKS ANYMORE BECAUSE YOU CAN MAKE THEM YOURSELF AT HOME.

preparation 10 minutes / **servings** 2

1 cup	(250 ml) 2% plain yogurt
1 cup	(250 ml) milk
1 cup	(140 g) fresh or thawed frozen fruit of your choice (raspberries, mangoes, strawberries, blueberries, peaches, etc.) (see Want it Creamier?)
	1 to 2 tbsp sugar

1 In a blender, purée all of the ingredients until smooth (see Feel the Strain).

2 Divide the yogurt drink between two large glasses. Serve immediately or pour into a bottle and refrigerate. If refrigerating, mix well before serving.

WANT IT CREAMIER?

Just toss a few banana slices into the blender with your fruit!

BANANA
AND MANGO

STRAWBERRY

RASPBERRY

Chocolate Marshmallow Sticks

DROP THESE CHOCOLATE-COVERED MARSHMALLOWS IN A MUG OF HOT COCOA, AND THEY'LL MELT RIGHT AWAY. MIGHT EVEN MELT THE HEART OF THE PERSON YOU WANT TO SHARE THEM WITH!

preparation 15 minutes / **cooking** 2 minutes
waiting 1 hour / **servings** 6

3 oz	(85 g) 56% dark chocolate or milk chocolate, chips or discs
6	large marshmallows (see Stay Mallow)
2 tbsp	chocolate candy sprinkles

1 In a measuring cup or microwave-safe glass, melt two-thirds of the chocolate (2 oz/55 g) in the microwave oven. Add the remaining chocolate and mix vigorously. The chocolate is now tempered (see Temper the Chocolate p. 166) and ready to use.

2 Line a plate with a square of parchment paper. Insert a wooden popsicle stick into each marshmallow.

3 Dip one marshmallow at a time in the chocolate, letting some of the excess drip off. Place the marshmallows upright on the plate. Garnish with the candy sprinkles. Let sit until the chocolate has set, about 1 hour at room temperature or 15 minutes in the refrigerator.

4 The chocolate marshmallow sticks will keep for 1 week in an airtight container at room temperature.

STAY MALLOW

You can either use the homemade Vanilla or Raspberry Marshmallows found on pages 152 and 153, or store-bought ones.

Hot Chocolate

AFTER A FUN DAY PLAYING OUTSIDE, WARM UP WITH THIS COZY DRINK MADE WITH JUST A FEW SIMPLE INGREDIENTS.

preparation 5 minutes / **cooking** 10 minutes
servings 6

3 cups	(750 ml) milk	
2 tbsp	sugar	
1 tbsp	cocoa powder	
6 oz	(170 g) milk chocolate, chopped	

1 In a pot over medium-high heat, bring the milk, sugar and cocoa powder to a boil while whisking constantly. Remove from the heat.

2 Add the chocolate to the pot and let sit for 2 minutes without stirring. Whisk until the chocolate has completely melted.

3 Divide the hot chocolate among six mugs. Serve with chocolate marshmallow sticks (recipe opposite) or mini marshmallows, if desired.

ADDED MILK
You can find the milk powder that's used in this recipe in the baking aisle of most grocery stores.

Hot Chocolate Mix for Gifting

FOR A COOL GIFT IDEA, PUT ALL THE HOT CHOCOLATE INGREDIENTS IN A JAR. THE PERSON YOU GIVE IT TO WILL JUST NEED TO ADD WARM MILK AND STIR IT UP.

preparation 10 minutes / **servings** 14

1¼ cups	(130 g)	milk powder (see Added Milk p. 142)
½ cup	(105 g)	sugar
½ cup	(50 g)	cocoa powder
6 oz	(170 g)	64% dark chocolate, coarsely chopped
2 tsp		cornstarch

1 In a blender, grind all of the ingredients into a fine powder. The hot chocolate mix will keep for 2 months in an airtight container at room temperature.

GIFT LABEL
Make a label like this for the jar so your friend knows how to mix their tasty hot chocolate!

HOT CHOCOLATE MIX

TO _____

FROM _____

For 1 serving, warm ¾ cup (180ml) of milk with 3tbsp (45ml) of hot chocolate mix, and stir.

CHAPTER 05

YOUR FAVORITE CHAPTER:
DESSERTS

WE SAVED THE BEST FOR LAST! THESE RECIPES ARE GUARANTEED TO SATISFY YOUR SWEET TOOTH, SO BREAK OUT YOUR WHISK AND SPATULA AND GET READY TO BAKE SOME CAKE, COOKIES AND EVEN A CHOCOLATE PIZZA WITH US! YOUR PATIENCE HAS BEEN REWARDED.

HOW TO **FOLD** INGREDIENTS

1 Hold a spatula in one hand, and hold the bowl with the other.

2 Make an up-and-down movement by gently folding the mixture over itself. With the other hand, rotate the bowl a quarter turn with each movement of the spatula. (If you're very gentle, you won't squish the air bubbles out of the whipped cream and your ice cream will be as fluffy as a cloud!)

3 Slowly and softly transfer your mixture into the container.

Cheesecake Ice Cream

BY MIXING CREAM CHEESE WITH ICE CREAM, YOU'RE PRETTY MUCH EATING CHEESECAKE IN A CONE—AND THERE'S NOTHING WRONG WITH THAT!

preparation 20 minutes / **freezing** 8 hours
makes about 5 cups (1.25 L)

1 block	(9 oz/250 g) cream cheese, softened
1 tsp	(5 ml) lemon juice
1 can	(10 oz/300 ml) sweetened condensed milk
1 tsp	(5 ml) vanilla
1½ cups	(375 ml) 35% whipping cream
	Fresh strawberries, quartered, for serving
	Graham crackers, broken, for serving

1 In a food processor, cream (see Glossary p. 191) the cream cheese with the lemon juice. Add the condensed milk and vanilla. Mix to combine. During this step, stop the food processor and remove the lid. Using a spatula, scrape down the sides of the food processor. Replace the lid and continue to mix until smooth. Set aside.

2 In a bowl, whisk the 35% cream with an electric mixer on medium speed until semi-stiff peaks form.

3 Using a spatula, gently fold the cream cheese mixture into the whipped cream until smooth. Transfer to an airtight container. Freeze for 8 hours or until the ice cream is firm.

4 Before serving, let the ice cream sit out at room temperature as needed to soften slightly. Place scoops of ice cream in a bowl. Garnish with strawberry wedges and pieces of graham cracker. Serve immediately.

VANILLA ICE CREAM

To make vanilla ice cream, whisk 2 cups (500 ml) 35% whipping cream and 1 tbsp (15 ml) vanilla with an electric mixer until semi-stiff peaks form. Fold in 1 can (10 oz/300 ml) sweetened condensed milk. Transfer to an airtight container. Freeze for 8 hours or until the ice cream is firm.

THESE TARTLETS ARE "À LA MODE"!

"À la mode" is a French expression that means a dessert is served with ice cream on top!

RICARDO

Quick Crispy Tartlets

EVEN THOUGH THEY'RE MADE USING WONTON WRAPPERS, YOU'LL JUST HAVE TO TRUST US THAT THESE MINI TARTS WON'T TASTE LIKE WONTON SOUP!

preparation 15 minutes / **cooking** 8 minutes
cooling 35 minutes / **makes** 1 dozen

12	frozen square wonton wrappers, thawed
2 tbsp	butter, melted
2 tbsp	sugar
¼ cup	(60 ml) raspberry jam or dulce de leche (see What's Dulce De Leche?)
	Vanilla ice cream, for serving
	Fresh raspberries, for serving (optional)

1 With the rack in the middle position, preheat the oven to 375°F (190°C).

2 On a work surface, using a pastry brush, spread (see Glossary p. 193) the wonton wrappers on both sides with the butter. Sprinkle both sides with the sugar. Line (see Glossary p. 191) each cavity of a non-stick muffin pan with a sugared wonton wrapper. Place 1 tsp (5 ml) of the jam or dulce de leche in each wrapper.

3 Bake for 8 to 10 minutes or until the tartlets are nicely browned. Remove from the oven and let cool on a wire rack for 5 minutes. Unmold the tartlets while they are still warm. Let cool completely, about 30 minutes.

4 Garnish each tartlet with ice cream and raspberries, to taste.

WHAT'S DULCE DE LECHE?

It's like a yummy milk jam. Sugar is mixed with milk and simmered until it thickens and turns into a golden caramel color. You can usually find it near the jams and jellies in the grocery store.

MORE WAYS TO USE A MUFFIN PAN

↓

You can use your muffin pan to:

> **Make individual portions of mac and cheese**

> **Bake mini omelets in the oven**

> **Put burger and taco toppings in their own compartments**

> **Separate your favorite candies**

Chocolate Popsicles

YOU DON'T HAVE TO WAIT FOR SUMMER TO ENJOY AN ICE POP! MAKE THEM AT HOME, AND YOU'LL SEE HOW FUN THEY ARE WHETHER YOU'RE IN A SWIMSUIT OR A COZY SWEATER.

preparation 15 minutes / **cooking** 12 minutes
freezing 6 hours / **makes** 8, depending on the mold

2¼ cups	(560 ml)	milk
1 tsp	(5 ml)	vanilla
½ cup	(105 g)	sugar
2 tbsp		cocoa powder
1 tbsp		cornstarch
½ tsp		salt
2 oz	(55 g)	milk chocolate, chopped

1 In a pot over medium heat, bring the milk and vanilla to a boil. Keep an eye on the pot to make sure the mixture doesn't boil over.

2 Meanwhile, in a bowl, whisk together the sugar, cocoa powder, cornstarch and salt. Stir in the chocolate.

3 Pour half of the hot milk mixture in the bowl and whisk until the chocolate has melted. Pour the chocolate mixture into the pot of remaining milk.

4 Bring the mixture to a boil over medium heat, stirring constantly. Carefully pour the mixture into a measuring cup (see A Zero-Mess Trick p. 151).

5 Pour the mixture into a popsicle mold. Firmly tap the mold on the counter to remove any air bubbles. Insert a popsicle stick in the center of each popsicle.

6 Freeze for 6 hours or until the popsicles are set. To help with unmolding the popsicles, first run the bottom of the mold under warm water.

ARTS & CRAFTS BREAK!

Using wooden ice cream sticks to make these ice pops? If so, have some fun with the leftover sticks! Make a marionette puppet, an airplane or even a tiny house for your hamster. Let your creativity soar!

A ZERO-MESS TRICK

To make sure the kitchen counter (and your clothes!) stay mess free, use a measuring cup with a pouring spout to transfer the mixture into the ice pop mold.

VANILLA MARSHMALLOWS

To make vanilla marshmallows, swap the raspberry purée for ½ cup (125 ml) water and 1 tsp (5 ml) vanilla.

Raspberry Marshmallows

WITH THESE SIMPLE AND FLUFFY MARSHMALLOWS, EVERYTHING WILL SEEM AS SWEET AS A ROSY DREAM!

preparation 35 minutes / **cooking** 5 minutes
cooling 2 hours / **makes** 25

5 tsp	gelatin (or 2 packets)
½ cup	(125 ml) raspberry purée (see A Pretty Purée)
1 cup	(210 g) sugar
½ cup	(125 ml) clear corn syrup
¼ cup	(35 g) icing sugar
¼ cup	(35 g) cornstarch

1 Lightly oil an 8-inch (20 cm) square pan and line with plastic wrap. Lightly oil the plastic wrap.

2 In a small pot, sprinkle the gelatin over the raspberry purée. Let bloom for 5 minutes.

3 Add the sugar to the pot. Bring to a boil, stirring, just until the sugar and gelatin have dissolved. Remove from the heat and let cool for 5 minutes.

4 In a bowl, whisk the gelatin mixture and corn syrup with an electric mixer on low speed for 5 to 7 minutes or until the mixture is room temperature and soft peaks form (for best results, you can use a stand mixer if you have one). Spread the mixture out evenly (see Glossary p. 193) in the prepared pan. Using a spatula, smooth out the surface. Let cool at room temperature until the marshmallow mixture has set, about 2 hours.

5 In a bowl, combine the icing sugar and cornstarch. Sift through a sieve into another bowl.

6 Sprinkle some of the icing sugar mixture over a cutting board and the blade of a knife. Unmold the marshmallow mixture onto the cutting board. Cut into 25 large cubes.

7 Add the marshmallows to the bowl of remaining icing sugar mixture and gently coat. Place a few marshmallows at a time in the sieve and gently shake to remove any excess powder. The marshmallows will keep for 1 to 2 weeks in an airtight container at room temperature.

A PRETTY PURÉE

To make ½ cup (125 ml) raspberry purée, blend 1⅓ cups (165 g) thawed frozen raspberries until smooth. Strain through a sieve placed over a bowl, pressing on the purée with the back of a ladle. Compost the raspberry seeds.

Q&A TIME WITH QUENTIN

WHAT IS COMPOST ?

When you put food scraps into a compost bin, eventually they turn into humus (very different from the Hummus on p. 42!), which looks like dirt and is used to help plants grow. You can make compost at home by using a special bin, or check if your city or town collects food scraps for composting.

Here are some examples of organic materials that you can put in the compost bin:

> **Fruit and veggie peels**
> **Eggshells**
> **Bones and fat from meats**
> **Fish and seafood scraps**
> **Used coffee grounds and tea leaves**
> **Soiled paper and cardboard (like paper towels or facial tissues)**

153

2 CUPS

15 →

large marshmallows   small marshmallows

Marshmallow and Cookie Rice Cereal Roll

CRUMBS ARE MAGIC! TURN LEFTOVER CEREAL AND COOKIE CRUMBS INTO A DREAM DESSERT AND MAKE FOOD WASTE DISAPPEAR. ABRACADABRA!

preparation 10 minutes / **cooking** 5 minutes
cooling 30 minutes / **servings** 2 to 3

2 tbsp	butter
15	large white marshmallows (see Put Away Your Calculator!)
1 cup	(30 g) crispy rice cereal (Rice Krispies–style)
2	cream-filled chocolate cookies or cookies of your choice, broken

1 On a slightly wet work surface, place a 12-inch (30 cm) square of plastic wrap.

2 In a small pot over medium heat, melt the butter. Simmer gently for 15 seconds. Add the marshmallows and continue to cook, stirring constantly, until melted. Remove the pot from the heat.

3 Add the cereal and cookie pieces to the pot. Mix well.

4 Place the mixture along one end of the plastic wrap, leaving an empty border on both ends. Firmly roll the mixture up in the plastic wrap to form a log about 1½ inches (4 cm) in diameter.

5 Seal the roll by tying knots at either end of the plastic wrap. Let cool for 30 minutes at room temperature.

6 When ready to serve, remove the plastic wrap from the cereal roll. On the work surface, slice the roll. The cereal roll will keep for 1 week, well covered with plastic wrap, at room temperature.

PUT AWAY YOUR CALCULATOR!

If you have mini marshmallows, there's no need to count them! You'll need 2 cups (100 g).

PLAY WITH YOUR FOOD

CUT YOUR FRUIT INTO FUN SHAPES AND
MAKE SPECTACULAR FRUIT SKEWERS FOR DESSERTS
THAT ARE ANYTHING BUT ORDINARY!

WATERMELON PIZZA

FLORAL SKEWERS

Use any leftover watermelon scraps to make our Watermelon Lemonade Slush (p. 135).

Ask an adult help you peel a pineapple and then slice it into ½-inch (1 cm) discs. Use a flower-shaped cookie cutter to punch flower shapes out of the pineapple discs. Then use a smaller cookie cutter to punch out the center. You can create a colorful effect by adding a different fruit to the center hole! Try it with watermelon, honeydew and cantaloupe, or use a melon baller on them (it's like a tiny ice cream scoop to make balls of fruits and veggies). Then mix the shapes and fruits to create beautiful skewers!

For the watermelon pizza, you'll need to cut a large disc before slicing it into wedges. Decorate them with berries and other pieces of melon shaped with a cookie cutter.

Double Caramel Sundae

FOR A DESSERT THAT'LL MAKE THE WHOLE FAMILY DROOL, TRY A FUN SWEET AND SALTY COMBO LIKE PRETZELS AND ICE CREAM!

- -

preparation 25 minutes / **cooking** 12 minutes
cooling 20 minutes / **servings** 4

PRETZEL-PEANUT CRUNCH

⅓ cup	(30 g) broken small pretzels (see Demolition Time)
2 tbsp	salted roasted peanuts, chopped
2 tbsp	brown sugar
2 tbsp	butter, melted
1 tbsp	unbleached all-purpose flour

SUNDAE

½ cup	(125 ml) store-bought caramel
2 cups	(500 ml) caramel ice cream, or more to taste
8	small pretzels, to decorate

PRETZEL-PEANUT CRUNCH

1 Place four sundae cups or glasses in the freezer until ready to serve.

2 With the rack in the middle position, preheat the oven to 350°F (180°C). Line a baking sheet with a silicone mat or parchment paper.

3 In a bowl, combine all of the ingredients. Spread the mixture out on the baking sheet.

4 Bake for 12 minutes, stirring halfway through cooking. Remove from the oven and let cool completely on the baking sheet, about 20 minutes. Coarsely crumble.

SUNDAE

5 Place the caramel in a small glass bowl. Heat in the microwave oven for a few seconds until warm and runny.

6 Place ¼ cup (60 ml) of the ice cream into each chilled glass. Top with 1 tbsp (15 ml) of the warm caramel and 2 tbsp of the crunch mixture. Repeat these layers a second time, finishing off with the crunch. Decorate with the pretzels and serve immediately.

DEMOLITION TIME

You can crush pretzels by putting them in a resealable plastic bag and then smashing them with a rolling pin. You can also crush them in a small food processor or blender.

PRETZEL CRUNCH

THE QUICKEST DESSERT IN THE WORLD

GOT A SWEET TOOTH? IT CAN'T WAIT! GRAB A MUG FROM THE CABINET AND BAKE ONE OF THESE MICROWAVE DESSERTS. THE LONGEST STEP IS CHOOSING A RECIPE!

MONKEY BREAD
PICK IT APART
LIKE A MONKEY WOULD

160

BANANA BREAD

FOR DESSERT, A SNACK, OR EVEN BREAKFAST...

A BROWNIE

FOR THAT HIT OF CHOCOLATE

STICKY TOFFEE PUDDING

IT'S OH-SO GOOEY AND COMFORTING!

Sticky Toffee Pudding in a Cup

preparation 5 minutes / **cooking** 1 minute
cooling 5 minutes / **serving** 1

CAKE

3 tbsp	unbleached all-purpose flour
1 tbsp	brown sugar
¼ tsp	baking powder
1 tbsp	butter, softened
2 tbsp	(30 ml) milk

SYRUP

3 tbsp	(45 ml) maple syrup
1 tbsp	(15 ml) water

CAKE

1 In a 1½-cup (375 ml) microwave-safe mug, combine the flour, brown sugar, baking powder and butter with a fork until the butter forms pea-sized pieces. Add the milk and mix until smooth.

SYRUP

2 In a small bowl, combine the maple syrup and water. Pour over the batter in the mug. Place the mug on a microwave-safe plate to catch any overflow as the pudding cooks.

3 Cook in the microwave oven for 1 minute. Depending on the microwave, continue to cook for 15 to 20 seconds or until a toothpick inserted in the center of the cake comes out clean. Remove from the microwave and let cool for 5 minutes before eating.

Monkey Bread in a Cup

preparation 20 minutes / **cooking** 1 minute
cooling 5 minutes / **serving** 1

DOUGH

¼ cup	(40 g) unbleached all-purpose flour
1 tsp	sugar
¼ tsp	baking powder
⅛ tsp	baking soda
¼ cup	(60 ml) 2% plain Greek yogurt

COATING

1 tbsp	butter
4 tsp	brown sugar
2 tsp	sugar
¼ tsp	ground cinnamon

DOUGH

1 In a bowl, combine the flour, sugar, baking powder and baking soda with a fork. Add the yogurt and mix until smooth. Remove the dough from the bowl and shape into a disc (see Glossary p. 191) with your hands.

2 On a lightly floured work surface, cut the disc of dough into eight equal pieces. Shape each piece into a ball. Set aside.

COATING

3 In a small glass bowl, melt the butter in the microwave oven. Set aside.

4 In another small bowl, combine the brown sugar, sugar and cinnamon.

5 Dip one ball of dough at a time in the melted butter, then coat with the brown sugar mixture.

6 Place the dough balls in a 1½-cup (375 ml) microwave-safe mug (preferably with angled sides) as you go. Pour any remaining brown sugar mixture and melted butter over the dough balls in the mug.

7 Cook in the microwave oven for 1 minute. Remove from the microwave and let cool for 5 minutes before eating.

Banana Bread in a Cup

preparation 10 minutes / **cooking** 1 minute
cooling 5 minutes / **serving** 1

½	very ripe banana
1 tbsp	brown sugar
1 tbsp	(15 ml) vegetable oil
¼ cup	(40 g) unbleached all-purpose flour
¼ tsp	baking soda
1 pinch	ground cinnamon
10	chocolate chips (optional)

1 In a 1 ½-cup (375 ml) microwave-safe mug, mash the banana and brown sugar with a fork. Add the oil and mix well. Add the flour, baking soda and cinnamon. Mix just until the dry ingredients are moistened (see Glossary p. 192). Stir in the chocolate chips.

2 Cook in the microwave oven for 1 minute or until a toothpick inserted in the center comes out almost clean. Remove from the microwave and let cool for 5 minutes before eating.

Brownie in a Cup

preparation 5 minutes / **cooking** 40 seconds
cooling 5 minutes / **serving** 1

¼ cup	(40 g) unbleached all-purpose flour
1 oz	(30 g) dark chocolate, chopped
2 tbsp	brown sugar
1 tbsp	cocoa powder
2 tbsp	butter, melted
1 tbsp	(15 ml) milk
1	egg yolk

1 In a 1½-cup (375 ml) microwave-safe mug, combine the flour, chocolate, brown sugar and cocoa powder with a fork. Add the butter, milk and egg yolk. Mix just until the dry ingredients are moistened.

2 Cook in the microwave oven for 40 seconds or until a toothpick inserted in the center of the brownie comes out with a few crumbs attached and not completely clean. Remove from the microwave and let cool for 5 minutes before eating.

FEELING GENEROUS?

This recipe yields one serving. If you want to make another one for a friend, you'll have a fun math challenge on your hands! To make two brownies, use one whole egg. Beat it gently with a fork and then distribute it evenly between two mugs and mix with the other ingredients. But remember, no matter how many servings you make, cook only one mug at a time in the microwave!

SAFETY 101

Choose a mug that can hold at least 1½ cups (375 ml) to avoid overflowing. Your dessert will be very, very hot when it comes out of the microwave—be sure to wait 5 minutes before eating.

163

BITE INTO THIS COOKIE DOUGH

Cookie Dough You Can Eat with a Spoon

DID YOU KNOW THAT YOU SHOULD NEVER EAT RAW COOKIE DOUGH? EXCEPT FOR THIS RECIPE, MADE WITH HEAT-TREATED FLOUR THAT'S SAFE TO EAT!

- -

preparation 15 minutes / **cooking** 1 minute
cooling 20 minutes / **makes** 1½ cups (375 ml)
freezes well

½ cup	(75 g) unbleached all-purpose flour
¼ cup	(55 g) unsalted butter, softened
¼ cup	(55 g) brown sugar
¼ tsp	salt
¼ tsp	(1 ml) vanilla
1 oz	(30 g) milk or dark chocolate, chopped

1 Place the flour in a glass bowl. Cook the flour in the microwave oven for 1 minute, stirring every 15 seconds. Let cool completely, about 20 minutes.

2 In a bowl, cream the butter, brown sugar, salt and vanilla with a wooden spoon (see Double Chocolate). Stir in the cooled flour and chopped chocolate.

3 Shape into balls with your hands, using 1 tsp of the dough for each one, or crumble directly over ice cream.

4 The cookie dough will keep for 1 week in an airtight container in the refrigerator or for 3 months in the freezer.

- -

DOUBLE CHOCOLATE
If you want a chocolate dough, add 1 tbsp cocoa to the butter and brown sugar mixture.

For a colorful cookie dough, you can replace the chocolate with 2 tbsp colored sprinkles!

GERM-FREE FLOUR
To safely enjoy raw cookie dough, your flour needs to be heat treated—or in other words, cooked! Flour is a raw food that comes from grains. Sometimes it can get dirty from bacteria in the dirt, water or even animal droppings (yuck!) in the field. But don't worry: heat kills those germs to make the flour safe to eat! For this recipe, you can cook the flour in the microwave.

Cruncy Chocolate Cereal Treats

EVEN TASTIER THAN REGULAR POPCORN, THESE SWEET CLUSTERS WILL GIVE YOU THE ENERGY YOU NEED TO WIN EVERY ROUND OF YOUR FAVORITE BOARD GAME!

preparation 20 minutes / **cooking** 2 minutes
waiting 1 hour / **makes** 2 dozen

6 oz	(170 g) 56% to 70% dark chocolate, chopped
1 cup	(30 g) nut-free round oat cereal (Cheerios-style) (see Mix it Up! p. 167)
½ cup	(15 g) crispy rice cereal (Rice Krispies–style)
½ cup	(15 g) cornflake cereal (Corn Flakes–style)

1 Line a baking sheet with a silicone mat or parchment paper.

2 Place 4 oz (115 g) of the chocolate in a glass bowl. Melt the chocolate over a pot of simmering water or in the microwave oven. Off the heat, add the remaining chocolate to the bowl and mix vigorously until melted. The chocolate is now tempered and ready to use (see Temper the Chocolate).

3 Add the cereal to the bowl of chocolate and mix until well coated. Using a 1 tbsp (15 ml) ice cream scoop, shape the mixture into little mounds and place on the baking sheet.

4 Let sit at room temperature for 1 hour or until the chocolate has completely set. The cereal treats will keep for 2 weeks in an airtight container at room temperature.

TEMPER THE CHOCOLATE

This method is used to make sure your chocolate stays smooth and shiny and doesn't turn white as it hardens. Check out step 2 to see how it's done!

CHOMP!
CHOMP!
CRUNCH!

MIX IT UP!

If you don't have the cereal that's listed in the ingredients, you can use whatever you have in your pantry! Just make sure you have a total of 2 cups of cereal.

ESSENTIAL BAKING TOOLS

TO MIX
Mixing bowls, a wooden spoon, whisk, spatula, hand mixer.

TO MEASURE
Measuring cups for dry ingredients, measuring jug for wet ingredients, measuring spoons, a kitchen scale.

dry ingredients   wet ingredients

TO BAKE
A cake pan, baking sheet, muffin tin, square baking dish, oven mitts.

DESSERT HERO

ARE YOU BAKING DESSERT FOR YOURSELF ONLY?

YES   NO

IS A GROWN-UP NEARBY TO HELP YOU USE THE OVEN?

NO   YES

Make a Brownie in a Cup.
(p. 163)

DO YOU HAVE ICE CREAM?

YES   NO

GREAT!

Bake the Fruit and Chocolate Cookies.
(p. 185)

BAKED AND EATEN, IN A FLASH!

Make a few
EASY ICE CREAM SUNDAES!

CHECK TO SEE IF YOU HAVE A JAR OF CHOCOLATE SPREAD TO SATISFY YOUR SWEET TOOTH...

Chocolate Mousse

ARE CHOCOLATE CLOUDS REAL? WITH THIS
LIGHT-AS-AIR MOUSSE, YOU'LL DEFINITELY BE
ON CLOUD 9 AFTER JUST ONE BITE!

preparation 15 minutes / **cooking** 3 minutes
chilling 9 hours / **servings** 4

1¼ cups	(310 ml)	35% whipping cream
3½ oz	(100 g)	64% to 70% dark chocolate, chopped
¼ cup	(35 g)	icing sugar
½ tsp	(2.5 ml)	vanilla

1 In a small pot, bring ½ cup (125 ml) of the 35% cream to a boil. Remove from the heat.

2 Add the chocolate to the pot and let melt for 1 minute without stirring.

3 Add the remaining cream, the icing sugar and vanilla to the pot. Whisk until smooth. Pour into a bowl. Cover with plastic wrap directly on the surface of the chocolate cream. Let cool. Refrigerate for 8 hours or overnight.

4 In the bowl, whisk the chocolate cream with an electric mixer on medium speed until semi-stiff peaks form. Divide the mousse among four cups or ramekins. Cover and refrigerate for 1 hour.

5 The chocolate mousse will keep for 3 days in the refrigerator.

WHAT'S THAT PERCENTAGE?

The percentage (%) you see on a dark chocolate bar tells you how much cocoa is inside. The rest is cocoa butter and sugar. The more cocoa, the less sweet it is, but a lot of cocoa works perfectly in a mousse like this one!

MOUSSE FOR ALL!

FREEZER FRIENDS

Choose whatever frozen fruit you have on hand to create different flavor combos for your pudding cake:

> Mango-raspberry
> Strawberry-rhubarb
> Cherry-peach
> Peach-blueberry

Fruit Pudding Cake

YOU WON'T BE MISSING YOUR FAVORITE BERRIES DURING WINTER, BECAUSE YOU CAN MAKE THIS PUDDING CAKE USING FROZEN BLUEBERRIES AND RASPBERRIES!

preparation 25 minutes / **cooking** 1 hour
servings 4 to 5

1 cup	(210 g) sugar
2 tsp	cornstarch
2 cups	(280 g) frozen blueberries (see Freezer Friends p. 172)
2 cups	(250 g) frozen raspberries
¾ cup	(115 g) unbleached all-purpose flour
1 tsp	baking powder
6 tbsp	(85 g) unsalted butter, softened
1	egg
½ tsp	(2.5 ml) vanilla
¼ cup	(60 ml) milk

1 With the rack in the middle position, preheat the oven to 350°F (180°C).

2 In an 8-cup (2 L) soufflé dish (see Dish or Pot?), combine ½ cup (105 g) of the sugar with the cornstarch. Add the fruit and mix well. Set aside.

3 In a bowl, combine the flour and baking powder.

4 In another bowl, cream the butter and remaining sugar with an electric mixer on low speed for 2 minutes. Add the egg and vanilla. Mix until smooth. Stir in the dry ingredients, alternating with the milk. Spread the batter over the fruit in the baking dish. Place the dish on a baking sheet to catch any overflow as the cake cooks.

5 Bake for 1 hour to 1 hour 15 minutes or until a toothpick inserted in the center of the cake comes out clean. Remove from the oven and let cool slightly on a wire rack. The cake can be eaten hot or cooled.

DISH OR POT?

You can swap the soufflé baking dish for a stainless steel pot that's 7 inches (18 cm) wide and can hold 8 cups (2 L). Just make sure the handle is ovenproof!

FROZEN VS FLASH FROZEN

Think these two are the same thing? Not quite! Flash freezing is used in the food industry to freeze foods at very low temperatures—between -22°F and -58°F (-30°C and -50°C), and even less—really fast. This helps the food keep its texture, taste and nutrients.

Regular freezing involves your freezer at home, which is usually between 10.4°F and -0.4°F (-12°C and -18°C). It freezes foods much more slowly, creating ice crystals that can change the food's proporties. So if you put blueberries in the freezer, they'll be frozen, but not flash frozen like they are after they're picked in the field.

Birthday Cake

BAKING A CAKE FOR SOMEONE IS THE BEST GIFT YOU CAN GIVE THEM. AND THE BEST PART IS THAT YOU DON'T NEED TO WRAP IT!

- -

preparation 25 minutes / **cooking** 55 minutes
cooling 3 hours / **servings** 8 / **freezes well**

2 cups	(260 g) icing sugar
1½ cups	(225 g) unbleached all-purpose flour
3 tbsp	multicolored candy sprinkles, plus more for decorating
2 tsp	baking powder
1 tsp	salt
3	eggs
¾ cup	(180 ml) vegetable oil
¾ cup	(180 ml) milk
1 tsp	(5 ml) vanilla
1	recipe Vanilla Frosting (p. 179)

1 With the rack in the middle position, preheat the oven to 325°F (165°C). Butter the sides of an 8-inch (20 cm) springform pan (see Glossary p. 193) and line the bottom with parchment paper.

2 In a bowl, combine the icing sugar, flour, sprinkles, baking powder and salt.

3 In a large bowl, whisk the eggs, oil, milk and vanilla with an electric mixer on low speed for 1 minute. With the machine running, stir in the dry ingredients. Spread the batter out in the prepared pan.

4 Bake for 55 minutes to 1 hour or until a toothpick inserted in the center of the cake comes out clean. Remove from the oven and let cool on a wire rack. Unmold and let cool completely, about 3 hours.

5 Place the cooled cake on a serving dish. Using a spatula, spread the frosting over the top of the cake. Decorate with sprinkles.

6 The cake will keep for 3 days, covered, at room temperature.

MY BIRTHDAY
(SO NOBODY FORGETS IT!)

THERE'S A HIGH CHANCE IT'LL BE RAINING SPRINKLES ON YOUR BIRTHDAY!

TOTALLY
FLUFFY

Carrot Cake Cupcakes

THE BEST THING ABOUT CARROT CAKE IS THE CREAM CHEESE FROSTING, OF COURSE. DON'T WORRY—YOU HAVE OUR PERMISSION TO LOAD UP ON IT!

preparation 25 minutes / **cooking** 20 minutes
cooling 1 hour / **makes** 9 / **freezes well**

1 cup	(150 g) unbleached all-purpose flour
1½ tsp	baking soda
½ tsp	ground cinnamon
¼ tsp	ground nutmeg
¾ cup	(160 g) brown sugar
¼ cup	(60 ml) vegetable oil
½ tsp	(2.5 ml) vanilla
1	egg
¼ cup	(60 ml) milk
¾ cup	(100 g) finely grated carrots
1	recipe Cream Cheese Frosting (p. 179)

1 With the rack in the middle position, preheat the oven to 350°F (180°C). Line a pan with nine silicone or paper liners.

2 In a bowl, combine the flour, baking soda and spices.

3 In another bowl, whisk together the brown sugar, oil, vanilla and egg until smooth. Stir in the dry ingredients, alternating with the milk. Add the carrots and mix well. Divide the batter among the muffin cups.

4 Bake for 20 minutes or until a toothpick inserted in the center of the muffins comes out clean. Remove from the oven and let cool completely on a wire rack, about 1 hour, before unmolding.

5 Top the cooled muffins with the frosting. The cupcakes will keep for 3 days, covered, in the refrigerator.

CARROTS FOR DESSERT? WHY NOT!

THE ICING ON THE CAKE

FROSTING IS JUST AS IMPORTANT AS THE CAKE ITSELF! WHETHER YOU MAKE IT WITH BUTTER, CREAM CHEESE, CHOCOLATE OR WHIPPED CREAM, THIS COATING IS WHAT MAKES A GOOD CAKE GREAT.

EXTREMELY CREAMY

TOTALLY DELICIOUS

Vanilla Frosting

THIS IS THE MOST BASIC OF FROSTINGS, BECAUSE IT'S MADE WITH SIMPLE PANTRY INGREDIENTS. THERE ARE SO MANY (SWEET) POSSIBILITIES OR WHAT TO PAIR THIS WITH!

preparation 10 minutes
makes about 2 cups (500 ml) or enough for an 8-inch (20 cm) cake or 12 cupcakes

¾ cup	(170 g) unsalted butter, softened
2 cups	(260 g) icing sugar
½ tsp	(2.5 ml) vanilla

1 In a bowl, cream the butter, icing sugar and vanilla with an electric mixer on low speed for 2 minutes. Increase the speed to medium and whisk until smooth and creamy.

Cream Cheese Frosting

USE THAT CREAM CHEESE YOU LOVE IN THIS ICING RATHER THAN ON YOUR USUAL MORNING BAGEL.

preparation 10 minutes
makes about 1¼ cups (310 ml) or enough for 9 cupcakes

5 oz	(140 g) cream cheese, softened
2 tbsp	butter, softened
1¼ cups	(165 g) icing sugar

1 In a bowl, cream the cream cheese and butter with an electric mixer on low speed for 2 minutes. With the machine running, gradually stir in the icing sugar. Increase the speed to medium and whisk until smooth and creamy.

SO SWEET

UNSALTED
In frosting, just like in most desserts, you'll notice that the recipe calls for unsalted butter. Its flavor is milder and less salty, perfect for baking!

Don't have softened butter? Cut up the amount you need into cubes, then heat them in the microwave for 5 or 6 seconds at a time until soft, but not melted!

CHOCOLATE FANATIC

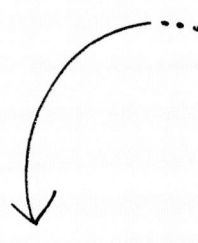

BEWARE OF FLAMES!

Never use aluminum foil in place of parchment paper in the microwave, because it can cause dangerous sparks!

Microwave Cookies

DID SOMEONE STEAL A COOKIE FROM THE COOKIE JAR? (WHO, ME? COULDN'T BE...) DON'T WORRY: YOU CAN HAVE A FRESH ONE READY IN MINUTES!

preparation 10 minutes / **cooking** 1 minute / **cooling** 5 minutes / **makes** 2

3 tbsp	(45 ml) chocolate-hazelnut spread
4 tsp	(20 ml) milk
¼ tsp	baking powder
⅓ cup	(50 g) unbleached all-purpose flour
2 tbsp	chocolate chips, plus more for garnish

1 Line two small microwave-safe plates with parchment paper.

2 In a bowl, combine the chocolate-hazelnut spread, milk and baking powder with a spoon until smooth (see Perfectly Baked). Add the flour and mix until combined. Stir in the chocolate chips.

3 Place half of the cookie batter on each plate. Flatten with your fingertips until the cookies are about 3 inches (7.5 cm) wide and ½ inch (1 cm) thick. Top with more chocolate chips.

4 Cook one cookie at a time in the microwave oven for 30 seconds. The cookie will be soft when it comes out of the microwave. Slide the cookie with the parchment paper off the plate and let cool for a few minutes before eating.

PERFECTLY BAKED

By mixing the baking powder with the wet ingredients, it'll be evenly distributed in the dough and the cookies will all rise to the same heights!

STOP
CANCEL

START
+30SEC.

Power

Timer

Time
Cook

0
Memory

7
GALLONS
That's how much milk a dairy
cow can produce each day—
sometimes even more!
We hope you have
enough cookies for
all of that milk!

Warning: chocolate eruption imminent!

Chocolate-Caramel Lava Cakes

OH NO! CARAMEL LAVA IS OOZING OUT OF YOUR CAKE AND SPREADING ACROSS YOUR PLATE! YOU (AND YOUR SPOON) NEED TO COME TO THE RESCUE!

preparation 25 minutes / **cooking** 14 minutes
waiting 5 minutes / **servings** 4 / **freezes well**

4 oz	(115 g) 70% dark chocolate, coarsely chopped
½ cup	(115 g) unsalted butter, cubed
2	eggs
½ cup	(105 g) sugar
¼ cup	(40 g) unbleached all-purpose flour
¼ cup	(60 ml) store-bought caramel, salted caramel or dulce de leche (see What's Dulce De Leche? p. 149)

1 With the rack in the middle position, preheat the oven to 350°F (180°C). Butter and flour four ¾-cup (180 ml) ramekins.

2 In a glass bowl set over a pot of simmering water or in the microwave oven, melt the chocolate with the butter. Mix well and let cool.

3 In another bowl, whisk together the eggs and sugar until smooth. Add the cooled chocolate mixture. Mix well. Stir in the flour until smooth.

4 Divide half of the batter among the ramekins. Spoon 1 tbsp (15 ml) of the caramel onto the center of the batter in the ramekins. Divide the remaining batter among the ramekins. Place the ramekins on a baking sheet. Cover and refrigerate or freeze at this point, if desired (see 3 Things to Remember).

5 Bake for 14 minutes or until the tops of the cakes are set and slightly browned. Remove from the oven and let rest for 5 minutes.

6 Run a thin blade between the cakes and the sides of the ramekins. Turn the hot cakes over onto plates to unmold.

3 THINGS TO REMEMBER

> Refrigerated cakes keep for 3 days.
> Frozen cakes keep for 3 months.
> You can bake a frozen cake without thawing it first—just add 5 or 6 minutes to the baking time. (That's 20 minutes in total!)

GO WITH THE FLOW

Just like lava that oozes from a volcano, lava cakes need to be soft in the center, so that the gooey caramel can easily ooze out!

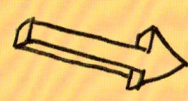

Fruit and Chocolate Cookies

THIS DESSERT IS LIKE CHOCOLATE FONDUE...ON A COOKIE! AND THE BEST PART IS THAT YOU'LL NEVER LOSE YOUR FRUIT AT THE BOTTOM OF THE FONDUE POT AGAIN. (YOU'RE WELCOME!)

preparation 20 minutes / **cooking** 12 minutes
cooling 5 minutes / **makes** 6

1 cup	(150 g) unbleached all-purpose flour
½ tsp	baking powder
¼ tsp	baking soda
6 tbsp	(85 g) unsalted butter, softened
⅔ cup	(140 g) brown sugar
1	egg
3 oz	(85 g) 64% to 70% dark chocolate, chopped or chocolate chips
6 tbsp	(90 ml) chocolate-hazelnut spread
2	small clementines, peeled and separated into segments
1	small banana, sliced into thin rounds
1¼ cups	(170 g) fresh raspberries or other fresh berries

1 With the rack in the middle position, preheat the oven to 375°F (190°C). Line a baking sheet with a silicone mat or parchment paper.

2 In a bowl, combine the flour, baking powder and baking soda.

3 In another bowl, cream the butter and brown sugar with an electric mixer on low speed for 2 minutes. Add the egg and mix for 1 minute. Using a wooden spoon, stir in the dry ingredients. Stir in the chocolate.

4 Shape into six balls, using about ¼ cup (60 ml) of the mixture for each one. Arrange, evenly spaced, on the baking sheet, without flattening the dough.

5 Bake for 12 minutes or until the cookies are golden around the edges but still very soft at the center. Remove from the oven and let cool on a wire rack for 5 minutes.

6 Using a small spoon, spread the center of each cooled cookie with 1 tbsp (15 ml) of the chocolate-hazelnut spread. Top with the fruit and serve.

YOUR FAVE FRUITS

CLEMENTINES

BANANA

RASPBERRIES

Gingerbread Cookies

EVER HEARD OF SPRING BREAK GINGERBREAD
COOKIES? HOW ABOUT FOR VALENTINE'S DAY
OR EASTER? OK, MAYBE NOT, BUT NOW THAT
YOU HAVE THIS RECIPE, THERE'S REALLY NO
REASON TO WAIT UNTIL CHRISTMAS!

preparation 25 minutes / **chilling** 1 hour
cooking 8 minutes per batch / **cooling** 30 minutes per batch
makes 4 dozen / **freezes well**

3 cups	(450 g) unbleached all-purpose flour
1 tbsp	ground ginger
1 tsp	baking soda
1 tsp	ground cinnamon
½ tsp	ground nutmeg
½ tsp	salt
¾ cup	(170 g) unsalted butter, softened
1 cup	(210 g) brown sugar
½ cup	(125 ml) molasses
1	egg
1	recipe Royal Icing

1 In a bowl, combine the flour, ginger, baking soda, cinnamon, nutmeg and salt.

2 In another bowl, cream the butter, brown sugar and molasses with an electric mixer on low speed for 2 minutes. Add the egg and mix well. With the machine running or with a wooden spoon, stir in the dry ingredients and mix until smooth.

3 Shape the dough into two discs with your hands. Cover with plastic wrap and refrigerate for 1 hour.

4 With the rack in the middle position, preheat the oven to 375°F (190°C). Line two baking sheets with silicone mats or parchment paper.

5 On a lightly floured work surface, knead one disc of dough at a time with your hands for 1 minute. Roll the dough out to ⅛ inch (3 mm) thick. Using cookie cutters of your choice, cut out the cookies. Place cookies of the same size on the same baking sheet, as the cooking time may vary between sizes.

6 Bake one sheet at a time for 8 minutes or until the edges of the cookies are golden. Let the cookies cool completely before icing, about 30 minutes.

7 Decorate the cookies with the royal icing.

ROYAL ICING

In a bowl, whisk 1 egg white and 1½ cups (195 g) icing sugar with an electric mixer on low speed for 2 minutes or until smooth. Transfer into a pastry bag fitted with a small plain tip for decorating the cookies. You could also use a butter knife to spread the royal icing over the cookies.

ALWAYS WAITING

If you need a third baking sheet for your cookies but you only have two, you need to wait 20 minutes for one to cool before you can use it again—otherwise the bottom of your cookies will cook faster than the tops. You can remove baked cookies with a spatula after they've cooled for 5 minutes.

Chocolate-Banana Pizza

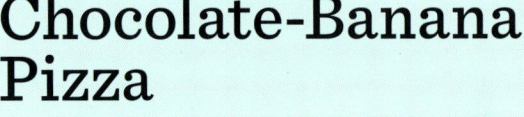

SINCE YOU'RE PREPARING PIZZA DOUGH FOR DINNER, YOU MIGHT AS WELL MAKE A SECOND BATCH FOR THIS CHOCOLATE AND BANANA VERSION—IT'S THE PEPPERONI AND CHEESE OF DESSERT!

preparation 20 minutes / **cooking** 20 minutes
servings 6

1	recipe Pizza Dough, risen in a skillet (p. 90)
1	small container (3½ oz/99 g) store-bought vanilla pudding
3 oz	(85 g) milk chocolate, chopped
2	ripe bananas, sliced into rounds

1 With the rack in the middle position, preheat the oven to 450°F (230°C).

2 With your fingertips, press the middle of the pizza dough so that the center is flat but the edge remains puffy all the way around.

3 Using a spoon, spread the vanilla pudding over the center of the dough only, avoiding the edge.

4 Bake for 20 minutes or until the dough is golden.

5 Remove the skillet from the oven. Immediately sprinkle 2 oz (55 g) of the chocolate over the vanilla pudding and wait 1 minute. Using the back of a spoon, spread the melted chocolate over the pudding, again avoiding the edge.

6 Slide the pizza from the skillet onto a cutting board.

7 Top the pizza with the banana slices. Sprinkle with the remaining chocolate. Cut into wedges and serve.

VERSATILE DOUGH
This is the same dough used for our Skillet Pizza (p. 89).

152 FEET
That's the length of the world's largest dessert pizza. It was made in Australia.

MAMMA MIA!

HERE'S A LIST OF DEFINITIONS THAT'LL COME IN HANDY
EACH TIME YOU READ A RECIPE AND SAY TO YOURSELF,
"WHAT DO THEY MEAN BY THAT?!"

A **Adjust the seasoning**
Tasting and then adding more salt and pepper as needed.

Airtight
Something that's leakproof once closed.

Al dente
Pasta that's firm when you bite into it, so neither too hard nor too soft.

B **Batch**
Amount of the same recipe that you bake in the oven one at a time, usually cookies or pastries.

Blanch
Dunking vegetables in boiling water for 1 or 2 minutes and then placing them in a bowl of ice water to stop the cooking process.

Boil (or bring to a boil)
Heating a liquid until it begins to form bubbles at the surface.

Broil
Cooking a dish under the broil setting in the oven until it browns.

Brown
Cooking something until the surface turns brown.

Brush
Dabbing something liberally using a brush.

GLOSSARY

C Capacity

The amount of ingredients a pot or pan can contain. Always test first using water.

Cooking water

Water that something has been cooked in.

Cream

Beating a mixture until it's smooth and creamy.

Crumble

Breaking something into crumbs using your fingers or the back of a fork.

Crush

Pressing something really hard.

D Disc

A ball of dough that's been slightly flattened. (Just don't put it into your grandparents' old CD player...)

Dissolve

Melting crystals, like sugar or salt, in liquid until they disappear.

Distribute

To dispense an ingredient evenly.

Drain

Separating and removing the liquid from the solids using a colander or fine mesh strainer.

Drizzle

Pouring something slowly.

F Finely chop

Cutting an ingredient (like herbs) into thin strips.

Flash frozen

A type of freezing method. (Learn the difference between freezing and flash freezing on p. 173.)

G Gradually

A little bit at a time.

I Incorporate

Adding and then mixing.

J Julienne

Cutting an ingredient into matchsticks.

L Line

Filling the cavities of a muffin pan with parchment paper or paper baking cups, or a baking sheet with parchment paper or aluminum foil, or a pie plate or dish with dough.

Low heat

Stovetop burner temperature between 1 and 3.

Lumps

Little clumps (yuck!), usually found in dough, due to insufficient mixing.

M Marinate
Soaking something in a liquid for a period of time to give it flavor.

Medium heat
Stovetop burner temperature between 4 and 6.

Medium-high heat
Stovetop burner temperature between 7 and 10.

Mix vigorously
Mixing something with lots of force.

Moisten
Wetting something very lightly.

P Parchment paper
A heat-resistant baking paper that keeps food from sticking to it.

Personal blender
A small blender that makes juices and smoothies, usually about one or two servings at a time.

Pinch
An amount of something that can be grasped between your thumb and index finger.

Pit
Removing the pit from a fruit.

Plastic wrap
Thin plastic used to cover food.

Preheated oven
An oven that's been turned and left on until the temperature you need has been reached (this usually takes about 15 minutes).

R Ramekin
A small porcelain dish used to make a single serving of something, usually baked in the oven.

Rest
To let something sit and wait (this means you can rest too!).

Ripe
When food is ready to be eaten!

Roughly chop
Cutting an ingredient into uneven pieces.

S Season
Adding flavor to a dish, particularly using salt and spices.

Seed
Removing the seeds from an ingredient.

Set
Cooling or freezing something until it's rigid and doesn't move.

Set aside
To put something to the side.

Shape
Forming something using your hands.

Shred
Pulling meats or cheese sticks into strands.

Silicone mat
A non-stick silicone sheet that's used as an eco-friendly replacement (you can use it again and again!) for parchment paper.

Simmer
Cooking slowly on medium-low heat.

Slice

Chopping something into thin, well, slices!

Soak

Submerging a dry ingredient in liquid until it absorbs the moisture, or dunking something in liquid until it's wet.

Soft peaks

When a mixture forms peaks that curve.

Soften

Making something soft, like leaving butter out to room temperature or cooking vegetables until they're tender.

Spread

Laying out ingredients evenly.

Springform pan

A cake pan that makes unmolding easy thanks to the bottom and sides that separate with a latch.

Sprinkle

Scattering an ingredient onto something.

Stiff peaks

When you whisk a mixture until it is firm, it can hold its shape and stand upright.

Stir

Mixing something softly.

T Temper

Letting something cool to room temperature.
Unless you live in an igloo, of course...

Transfer

Moving something from one container to another.

Trim

Preparing a food by removing parts (like bones and fat) that are inedible.

U Uniform

Things that are even or the same.

Unmold

Taking something out of a mold.

W Work surface

The part of the kitchen counter used to prepare your ingredients, or a cutting board if you're chopping something.

Y Yield

The amount or number of servings a recipe produces.

Z Zest

Grating the colorful exterior of citrus fruits like oranges, lemons and limes.

DRINKS

SNACKS

INDEX

MAIN DISHES

DESSERTS

A MESSAGE FOR YOUR GROWN-UPS

Thank you for being so inspirational to your kids, those of your friends and neighbours, and your nieces and nephews. During my visits to schools, I've witnessed how cooking can be beneficial to all children, particularly those who, for whatever the reason may be, don't conform to societal norms. Even if a recipe doesn't come together, they know they can try again next time. It's rewarding and concrete.

And a heartfelt thanks to all the budding chefs who have gravitated towards this book and will use it to begin their culinary journey. You've got this!

IT'S GOING TO BE
DELICIOUS!